# So Now You Know

*Best Wishes.*

*Barbie Smith*

*2009.*

WEBSITE: WWW. BARBIE SMITH.CO.UK

E.MAIK. barbie smith 123 @ AOLL.COM.

# So Now You Know

Barbie

2008

# So Now You Know

✿✿✿✿✿✿✿✿✿✿✿✿✿✿✿✿✿✿✿✿✿

# REMEMBERING BILL

✿✿✿✿✿✿✿✿✿✿✿✿✿✿✿✿✿✿✿✿✿

ACKNOWLEDGEMENTS.

I'd like to thank Graham, for being there.

To Lesley, for caring for me, and to Ryan my rock I could always lean on.

To Adam, my wonderful patient Editor, for his much needed advice and guidance.

A very special thanks to Elliott for his graphic design, and sheer dedication and patience with my tangled perplexity

Without you all, my story could not have been told.

## CHAPTER ONE

In a small house situated in Southampton, my parents were blessed with five children. My mother's maiden name was Florence Downer and my father was named Alfred Terrell. The eldest child was a girl, they named Joan and for quite a number of years she was called Betty.

The next three children were all boys, Len, Peter and Don, and last of all was another girl, the youngest of the brood, Barbara—and I am known as Barbie. Joan often had to look after us when we were young and what a task! We were all so full of boisterous fun. Joan, Len and Don had red hair whilst Pete and I favoured dark hair and were very much alike.

At times I was quite a tomboy, playing mostly with my three brothers. Joan was eight years my senior and was always combing my hair, polishing my shoes, and generally tidying me up. Oh dear, I hated this so much.

When out with my sister I certainly had to be little miss prim and proper, having to hold my head up high and pull my shoulders back. At times I became two personalities.

My dolls and pram, the family cat called Tibby, and later our dog Chum were my greatest loves. I would be locked in the land of make believe when playing with my treasures and they all had their turn at being pushed around in the dolls pram.

My imagination was very strong and I would act out quite bizarre situations. Many of my friends would play in the garden with me. I would pester my Mum for odds and ends of clothing and after practising we would put on a show for her and anyone else who would want to suffer. It was usually Mum, and she would painstakingly watch our efforts whilst ironing her mounds of clothes, smiling and laughing at the right time—we were only little tots.

Fresh milk would be delivered to the house daily, usually by horse and cart or with just the milkman pulling a cart. The dairy was only a little way from where we lived so there was always a lot of activity.

Early in the morning my brothers would have to run out with a bucket as the horses were coming out of the dairy. They would dispense their droppings on the roads and the boys would wait in anticipation to gather it all and shovel it in. This would be the manure for dad's garden.

Coal was delivered weekly but sometimes we would be able to collect a sack from the coal yard for a small charge, as it was not far from where we lived. The boys would have this task thrust upon them and they would have to wheel it in a barrow with small iron wheels that made a noisy rumbling din as it was pushed.

Most households would have coal fires and the smoke from these would cause a thick fog at certain times of the year making a hazy aura around the area when the street lamps were lit. It was eerie and spooky, but not to us as we didn't know any different.

As a form of protection, I can remember my mother wrapping scarves around our mouths if we had to go out.

Each evening the lamplighter would tour the streets lighting the lamps on his bicycle. He would carry a long thin cane with a connection on one end that would connect to the lamp and hey-presto the lamp would glow.

We loved to gather around the lamppost, as it would light up our area of play. The lamplighter would go from lamp to lamp without getting off his bicycle and if he was very good he did not stop.

The streets were our playgrounds. Out would come a large rope, which would be stretched from pavement to pavement. All the children would join in and skip and at times the odd parent would participate.

Sometimes we would sit on the curbs and play 'dibs'.
I think they are called 'five stones' now. This would go on for a long time, and many times we competed against one-another.

Tops were a favourite pastime. We would spin the little wooden tops with our hands to get them spinning or wrap the top around the string, which was part of the whip and then pull. Wow would it spin—and then the fun would begin...The top would spin along the road and then spin and spin on the spot but at this point you had to whip it again to keep it going—great fun.

Kites would come to the fore at certain times of the year, mainly when there was a good breeze. My brothers would get hold of some cane, if available, and split it down the middle to make the base for the frame. It would be tied together with string. Newspapers would be cut and then pasted to the frame with a paste made from flour and water. The tail then had to be made from a very long piece of string with rolled newspaper along it and a piece of rag as a tail. Around the front of the kite, three pieces of string would be attached from corner to corner to meet in the middle and this is where the main ball of string would be attached. If all the dimensions were right, the kite would be ready to fly high in the sky.

Hoops, some iron and some wooden, would pound down the streets when we ran and pushed them along with a stick of sorts. If the hoops were not available out would come an old wheel from a discarded bicycle.

One day when I was feeling a little adventurous I borrowed my friend's iron hoop and as I raced along the road—yes, it happened—over the top I went and ended up with a broken arm. Fortunately traffic was practically void where we lived.

Marbles were little round clay balls and would be played with at all times. We kept them in a little cloth bag pulled up with string and whenever the pavements were re-surfaced with tarmac, we would make little round indentations before it had really hardened to roll our marbles into. We would have to be a little way away from the hole and then roll them in. If they didn't quite reach, we would then use our fingers to scoop them along into the hole. The winner would get all the marbles.

As we got older we would play with 'aggets'. These were made of glass and were beautiful colours. The agget would be rolled along and then the opponent would roll one and try to hit it. If lucky, the agget was theirs.

Cigarette cards were a favourite with my brothers. Every packet of cigarettes had a card enclosed and they were very collectable. There were actually a series of various topics such as butterflies, soldiers through the ages, footballers, train, and many more. They would be catalogued and kept with any surplus being used to play the game of flicks.

In 'flicks', cards would be placed against the wall, and each player would flick a card to try to knock them down. The one that achieved this would claim the card. The art was in the flicking and the lads would become quite skilful at this.

'Leap-frog' would be great fun. A number of us would bend over in a line and one would leapfrog over each one.
The longer the line, the more fun would be had.

'Relievio' was a very boisterous game played mainly by the boys. One lad would bend over against a wall and one would run and jump on him the others would follow jumping on top until eventually they all fell over.

There was always a collection of sorts to enable us to play.
One of these was a small tin lid. A hole would be inserted in the middle and string would be pushed through and knotted. We would then stand it up and roll it along with the string.

Hand warmers were a must for the boys. They would get a small tin, pierce holes around it and then insert some rags and light it. String would be tied around the middle and they would then run along with smoke bellowing through the wind. Fortunately it did not last long. If the weather were cold, hands would then get warmed through.

Stilts were great fun. Two pieces of wood were needed, roughly long enough to reach your shoulders. On the inside of each piece, a block of wood would be placed at a suitable height where you would place your feet. You would then be able to proudly prance along, although most of the time you would fall off and land on the pavement. That did not deter you though, and up you would get to try again.

Bows and arrows were a firm favourite with the boys. For the bows, bendy branches would be collected from the hazel trees and string attached end to end so it formed a bow shape. The arrows were made, again, from tree branches but of a firmer kind. Out would come the pen-knives (all boys possessed a pen knife) and the end of the sticks would be sharpened to make a point with some chicken wire bound around to make it heavy. They were then ready for their Robin Hood games.

Catapults were also very popular and a 'Y' shaped piece of a branch was very sought after. A piece of rubber from an inner tube was cut to size and attached to the top part of the Y shape and then it was ready to ping.

Empty round tins, roughly the size of maybe today's baked bean tins, were used as a form of stilts. Off would come the label and the tin would be washed to be ready for the next stage. Two holes had to be bored into the top, and string was inserted into each side and knotted. It was then pulled up to form a loop. You would then place your feet on the cans hold the loops and walk.

The London fogs were very thick and many a song would be sung about these times. People would venture out and about and fumble their way around, it was very eerie. Today's children would love to endure this fog especially with the celebration of Halloween. What spooky fun they would have. Obviously we still have the odd fog, but they are very light in comparison and mostly surround areas near water. Today smoke rarely comes from the chimneys of houses and this was a big factor in causing the fogs we experienced. Smoke-free areas are to the fore in this day and age, with most homes centrally heated either by electricity or gas.

We missed the roaring fires in the grate and the glow of the embers in the evening. What we didn't miss though, was cleaning out the ashes in the morning—the dust it would leave on the furniture—and the yearly sweeping of the chimneys.

The chimney sweep would arrive and remove sacks of soot. We would run outside and wait until the brush poked out from the chimney—this would indicate that the job was near completion.

The housewife would then be left with the spring-cleaning task of the home. It would be dangerous if the chimneys were not regularly cleaned, as the soot would accumulate and it would easily catch fire. Flames would bellow up from the chimney and the fire brigade would have to be summoned. Sometimes it would be too late and the house would catch fire.

Fire engines really frightened me when I heard the clang of their big brass bell. I would run home as fast as I possibly could, I always thought they were heading for our house, although Mum was meticulous in having the chimney sweep visit regularly. It was a fear that never left me as a child.

Gas and electricity were in most homes to cook with or to light the bulbs in each room. This was paid for, by inserting money into a meter. We would love it when the gasman came and emptied it—piles of pennies would spill over on the table. He would count them and put them into little piles before sliding them into bags. We loved to watch. Sometimes there was money over which was given to Mum and maybe that day we would get a welcome treat.

CHAPTER TWO

The streets where we lived created a close community. The top of the road housed the 'Millers' a very nice reserved family. The 'Ketleys' and then our family the 'Terrells' followed them. Next, were the 'Scrivens' and then the 'Topleys' who were quite a large family. After a few years they moved out and the 'Griffiths' family moved in.

Next were the 'Woodhouses' and then the 'Browns'. Mr Brown had a parrot and he would place it in the front garden in a big cage. We would stop and chat to Polly; he was a lovely living feature of the community and caused a great joy to all who passed by.

The 'Gilberts' lived next door. Mrs Gilbert had lots of apple trees in her garden and in the season she would make succulent toffee apples which we would often buy on our visits if we were lucky to have pocket money to spare. If we didn't, maybe we would run errands for someone and they would reward us so that we could rush to get a toffee apple. Sometimes we would be lucky enough to get a doubler' it was two small apples on the stick.

On we go and it was then the 'Brewers' followed by the Smiths' and then the 'Shillabeers.' I could go on and on, this was only one side of the road; the other side of the road housed the 'Martins' opposite our house.

The 'Mac-Clennins' were next and then the 'House' family followed by the 'Warns' the 'Baileys' the 'Hardimans', 'Goodridges', 'Robinsons' and another 'Martin' family and so on and so on.

Southampton common was a place where we would play. Mum would fill bottles of lemonade made from lemonade-powder and water and off the family would go with my sister in charge. In the autumn we would play with all the mounds of leaves and the girls would create make-believe houses. The boys would gather the leaves in sacks, stack into their barrows full and wheel them home—again to rot down for dad's garden.

Other times the leaves we would gather from the common were used for Guy Fawkes Night, some for the stuffing of the guy and the rest for the bonfire. We loved the 5th of November. Nearly every garden had bonfires and the areas around would be a smoke-zone.

The man of the house would be in charge. We loved the fireworks and most of all, the sparklers. We would run from garden to garden enjoying each other's celebrations and watch the guys gradually disintegrate into the fires. Chestnuts were baked and potatoes would be black and charred from the fire. We would throw them from hand to hand until they were cooled. It was a great time, such fun.

Several celebrations were held yearly at the Common, where all the schools in Southampton would congregate. There would be mass country dancing, marching, waving flags, and singing patriotic songs, Empire Day was the main day for these celebrations and we were all very excited when this day arrived and could partake.

The Central Hall in Southampton was the venue for the Schools musical festivals. To us as children, it was a very impressive place. We would be in awe and very nervous, but very happy if our school came away with the cup. Sometimes we would compete at Bournemouth. This would be very exciting, as it would entail a bus ride.

As I became older, my ventures would allow me to play with friends at their houses. One of these friends was Edna Bailey who lived not far along the road from my house. Edna had six sisters and she was the youngest. Her older sisters mainly worked in Service locally as maids.

Often we would visit them to take clean clothes and goodies from their parents, and were rewarded with pennies or homemade cakes, so our visits were not a chore.

Edna became a very good friend and at times it seemed I was more at her house than I was at my own, especially school holidays and weekends. We had many treats from the sisters. She also had an auntie living in the household. Auntie did all the cooking she was quite an eccentric lady. Her clothes were styled back in the Victorian era, with layers of long black skirts, buttoned boots, and black tops up to her neck. Nothing was bared with the exception of her beautiful face. Auntie's hair was white and was pulled back in a bun.

Many trips were enjoyed visiting the theatre and pantomimes and to the cinemas for the Shirley Temple films etc.

People would stare at our escort as she was quite unique, but we were young and it did not mean a thing to us. Auntie was completely oblivious. She loved Edna and I believed she loved me too.

It was magic for me to go to the cinema. Excitement flowed through me as Auntie's hand plunged into the pocket of her full billowing black skirt and pulled out her worn purse. She clipped open the clasp and the pennies would tumble out for our sweets and ice cream. Oh the bliss, as this was not available in abundance at my home.

Edna was spoiled and I was heading that way too. More money was obviously in abundance compared to our household. I would earn a few coppers shopping for people otherwise I would have to be content with our weekly halfpenny.

We were friends all through our junior school days and as we progressed to the senior schools we saw less of each other. Edna was a year older than me and this is when we became more independent and spread our wings.

As children we were given a halfpenny each Friday this would have to last the week we were given a comic each and when read would exchange amongst each other and friends. Our halfpenny would have to stretch a long way, we would chase round to the little sweetshop called 'BON BONS'. The owners of the shop were very patient with the children. I remember staying and pondering for a very long time. I just had to get it right, get as much as I could for my money.

The jars were meticulously lined along the shelves, all full of mouth-watering sweets. Tiny acid drops, a sweet called hundreds and thousands, a sherbet dab, a sherbet fountain, liquorice strips, gob suckers, a surprise bag, and so much more. If we were lucky to have a penny to spend, the choice would widen. There would be a bag of chewing nuts, bars of toffee, liquorice- all sorts, caramels, succulent boiled sweets, chocolate bars—I could go on and on.

'Mrs Bon Bon' as we all lovingly called her is still living in the year 2005 at the wonderful age of 105 years. 'Bon Bons' was situated in Burgess Road in the middle of a row of shops.

'Greenwoods' was a cake shop. We didn't have the joy of going in there very often, only maybe for the odd loaf of bread, but we would stop and gaze at the wonderful array of cakes.

The 'Home and Colonial' was next. It was a very smart and well kept general store selling dairy products and cold meats etc. 'Wiffens Fish and Chips' was next and as children we loved this shop. Although our parents could not afford to buy the family fish and chips sometimes we would buy a bag of scraps. This was the odd bit of batter that came off the fish and if we were lucky a tiny bit of fish would be attached. At times we would be treated to a bag of chips. These would be put into a little greaseproof bag wrapped in newspaper.

'Mitchels' the vegetable shop was next, and then the fresh fish shop called 'Ghandi's'. Mum would buy all her fish from here we had a lot of fish in our diet. 'Wallers' followed, another grocery shop, I can remember they would put wooden barrels outside, these would be filled with sawdust and pomegranates, I guess the sawdust protected the fruit.

On we go, and next was the 'Bon-Bon' shop. Then Mr Stent the butcher, he had sawdust on the floor and the meat did not look appealing. He was a funny little man; we did not shop there.

There was a sweet shop next door, 'Bryants' which was quite posh and sold exotic chocolates on one side, and cigarettes and cigars, pipes and pipe tobacco which would be weighed on little scales. Then there was then a gap, which lead to the back entrance of Swaythling Senior School and then another vegetable shop called 'Newbolts'. They also sold groceries and had a delivery service…a boy on a bicycle.

The next shop was a man's outfitters run by Mr Pope.On we go and we come to the Hairdressers. Mr Lockyer was the proprietor of both the men's barbershop and a women's hairdresser the other side. Going on we come to the 'Green library' run by the family with the name of 'Green'. It was only small, but a very friendly place. We were also able to purchase stationary here.

Moulton and Wilton was another high class grocery store Mum would purchase her bacon and ham from here, and we would love to see the counter-hand slicing through the bacon on the hand operated machine. The ham was on the bone, a long thin knife would come out and slither through the joint, and the succulent meat would be purchased for my dad maybe for his tea, or for his sandwiches, or his lunch at work.

When we were children we never had this treat, but sometimes we would help ourselves to a little of it on our way home, Mum never found out. Sometimes Mum would purchase the large knucklebone that went through the joint, and also some bacon bones and then she would make some tasty pea soup… Scrumptious.

The Shoe menders were next. We would gaze through the window watching the snobs mending the boots and shoes.Then there was 'Gillies' the bakers where they baked all of their bread and cakes on the premises. The aroma was breath taking to us. Their bread so crusty, lardi-cakes so yummy and doughnuts so mouth watering. The Chemist was attached to the local doctors we would have to go up the stairs to sit in the waiting room, and wait to be called into the surgery. Then a very formidable man, Dr Seymour, with his spaniel dog lying at his feet, would greet us. I hated these visits he would be sitting on his very comfortable chair and peer over his glasses. Doctors did not have the friendly nature as they do today.

On we go to 'Fields' the ironmongers, then to 'Murdocks ' the haberdashery shop where we would purchase all our cottons…wools…knitting needles, etc. The off-licence run by the Lanhams was next, followed by another butcher's shop named Winteridge, this is where we would purchase our meat, and the butchers were a very jovial crowd. Then it was 'Contanchies', the bicycle shop and the locals would take their radio batteries there to be charged. These were called accumulators.

As we grew older we were treated to what we called the 'Two-penny Rush' and I would go there on a Saturday morning with my brother to watch a film. As you may perceive the cost was two-pennies and the rush was when we pushed to get a good seat. It usually was a cowboy film and the other film was a trailer, so-called because we had to leave it at an exciting point until the next week.

If the projector broke down which it often did we would all shout, hiss, bang the seats and generally cause a disorderly commotion. We were not disruptive, just a little rowdy until the film was showing again. The venue was usually a large hall and the one that we attended was the Swaythling Methodist Hall that had its own balcony.

Xmas would be an exciting time for us all, and Mum made it as magical as she could. A beautiful tree would stand proudly in the corner of the room. Pretty little ornaments adorned it, accompanied by little packets of chocolates and sweets, chocolate cigars, and packets of sweet cigarettes. There were fairies and little candles that would be lit on Christmas Eve; glass baubles would dangle with much grace. These were very old and came from my grand- mother's house. The tinsel would be draped among the branches and would sparkle and glisten. I would be mesmerized.

Xmas Eve was one time we would eagerly scamper to bed in anticipation. The joy of waking in the morning the stocking hung at the bottom of the bed, all bulgy and waiting to be plunged into with eager little hands. It was usually filled with apple nuts, tangerines and sweets, crayons and writing books and pencils.

We would try to crack the nuts with our teeth, we couldn't wait to go downstairs and use the nutcracker. We all had so much pleasure from our stockings. We could not leave the bed-room until we were called, but we were happy to wait with our stockings and our excitement would be building up.

Our present would be waiting for us; yes sometimes we only had the one special present from our parents accompanied by a mixture of small ones. The special one would be wonderful, something we had dearly wanted.

My present was usually a doll or a doll's pram. Mum would have all the clothes made for the doll (the doll was usually a baby replica) it certainly kept me quiet for a long time. I can remember Don with his mechano-sets, but cannot remember much about the older ones in the family.

When Don got out his mechano set he would patiently build and screw in the tiny screws. He had miniature tools to do this, and over the years he was able to add to it. He would make cranes that would actually lift up his miniature cars etc.

I would play with Don's toys and get as much joy as with my dolls. He wasn't interested in my dolls, but I did not mind that at all I had to make believe all on my own until I met with my friends.

Other toys I remember are spinning tops, and a Mickey and Minnie mouse made of tin with a barrel organ. Minnie would sit on top of the organ, and Mickey would be by the side, and it would look as though he was winding it, when we turned the key Minnie would dance to the barrel organ music.

We always had puzzles, snakes and ladders and playing cards. A new torch was a present the boys loved, they would put the torch under the chin light it, and when it was dark they would make gruesome faces on the wall, it always frightened me, and they loved that.

As we grew older maybe we would be lucky to have a little fairy cycle or a small car. Don would sit in his car and would have to pedal it along with his feet. Christmas of long ago will always be etched in my mind.

Our family home incorporated two bedrooms, and a bathroom and toilet on the upper floor. On the ground floor a sitting room, kitchen, and a large walk-in larder. Attached to the outside wall was a large lean-to, we called the shed. It had a stone floor and a door leading to the back garden and one leading to the front it served as a play area for the children, especially on a wet day. The mangle for the washing was housed here.

We enjoyed turning the handle on the mangle, Mum would fold the wet sheets and put them through the big rollers, a tin bath was at the bottom and this caught the water. The sheets would come out damp, and in a pressed condition, ready to hang on the long high line that was situated in the back garden. Her washing would be white and glistening, blowing in the breeze, and she would gaze proudly at her efforts.

The family disliked washdays it was a ritual for all women to wash the mounds of clothes on a Monday.

Mum would be out of bed by five in the morning after dad had brought her a cup of tea.

A brick boiler was situated in the kitchen, which was called the copper. A fire was lit underneath where all the rubbish was burned, including wood. This would heat the water and the clothes would be put inside the copper and boiled. A long wooden stick would have to be continually used, to steep the washing while it was boiling. It was a catastrophe if it boiled over onto the kitchen floor. If it ever did 'operation clean-up' was performed. If ever we children were around we would run as fast as we possibly could to get out of the situation.

After the washing had boiled, it was transferred to the sink where it was tediously rinsed in cold water several times. The final rinse was dipped in blue water after the insertion of a blue bag. This made the linen look sparkling white it was then mangled, some were starched, and then it would be put out on the line in the garden to sway in the breeze.

When dry, the laundry was sprinkled with water and rolled up tightly with the exceptions of the sheets—these had to be folded. As we knew how the system worked, we would scarper. Don was the fastest to run so it was usually left to me. My Mum was so meticulous—out would come the glistening snowy white sheets and we would have to hold two corners whilst Mum would hold the other two and then the pulling would begin. Again it had to be folded, and yet more pulls. The ends had to be put together precisely, and if it weren't then the process would have to be tediously repeated again and again until it was right. We would be so impatient, and could not go to play until all sheets were properly folded.

Ironing was usually sorted the next day, and again it took a long time. The irons were actually solid iron and very heavy.

My mother heated hers over the gas flames on the stove, and she would spread thick blankets over the table, the ironing would then begin.

Sewing jobs would be put aside and it wasn't long before a pile had accumulated. The sewing box would come out in the evening, and my Mum would sit and sew and repair and darn the socks.

We did not live in a throw away society, that came in later years. All these very hard tasks had to be done on top of cleaning shopping and looking after the children.

As the boys grew older, they would entertain Mum with all sorts of mad tricks with singing and dancing and mimicking. While she was in the process of ironing Mum would lean on the table and laugh and laugh and her ironing would stop. I realise now it was good therapy for my Mum, who worked so hard. She was so lovely and had a wonderful sense of humour, with an infectious laugh. This has carried on through the family.

Our home was spotlessly clean, and it is only in adulthood that I realised how very hard my mother had worked to look after her family.

A black range was situated in the living room, and there was always a glowing fire, which would be lit in the early hours of the morning. We would jump out of our beds scurry down the stairs to the comfort of a lovely warm and welcome fire. Before this could happen, Mum had to clean out the ashes of the previous day, and black- lead the stove till it shone and sparkled.

A little brass tap was attached where there was a compartment for water next to the oven.

The hearth was white and again that had to be whitened with a hearthstone every day. This was about four inches long and about three inches in width with a depth of about two inches. It was a very hard chalk like substance that had to be damped and rubbed all over the hearth. Again this was also a daily ritual to the front doorstep.

When it was dry the hearth and step would be pure white— quite a feat when one is tackling black and white cleaning materials in the same area. Every morning without fail, this was our greeting—a big glowing fire and everything scrupulously clean. We were quite unaware of all the effort that had gone into it. I realise now how lucky we were.

Breakfast would be the first meal of the day and would usually consist of porridge which had to be made early in the morning as the oats were steamed in a two-part saucepan. The oats would be put in the top half and the water that steamed it would be on the bottom, the steaming hot porridge was absolutely delicious, and big bowls of it would be presented at the kitchen table.

We were not allowed to eat in the sitting room as this had to be kept as clean as possible. To give us warmth on a cold winter's morning, Mum would light the gas on the stove and it would soon warm up.

Once the older children had gone to school, the youngest

would have to be looked after by Mum, we all started our school life at the age of five years there were no nursery schools.

My mother would carry out shopping on a daily basis. The first visit would be to the vegetable shop for her fresh veg. My father would grow most of our vegetables in the garden, but at times it needed to be supplemented by the shop, I can remember having to shop for a pennyworth of potherbs. This consisted of carrots, onions, turnips and swede etc. Obviously these were some of the ingredients for the stew, or soup pot.

The baker was always on the list, where lovely fresh bread was purchased, and then it was onto the butchers where a great deal of picking and selecting of the best of the meats took place. We ate meat every day—it was a cheaper commodity than it is now. Chicken and turkey was a luxury and only eaten at Christmas time.

We looked forward to teatime when the fire would bring forth a big warm glow. Out would come the toasting fork and the children would toast the bread. Butter would be spread upon it or lovely beef dripping dusted with salt, scrumptious.

There were odd times when the muffin man would walk the streets. We would hear the clang of his bell, and if we were lucky and there was money in the pot we would have toasted crumpets as well. Teatime was the last meal of the day. Bathtime would be in a tin bath in front of a lovely fire, and we were then wrapped in white fluffy towels and after engulfing a steaming mug of cocoa with our hands, we were ushered to bed.

If it were wintertime we would find a hot builder's brick wrapped in a soft flannel material inside our beds, and after it was removed we would leap between the beautiful crisp white sheets. Stories were then told and I can remember being the 'main story teller' to Don.

I had a strong imagination and as I progressed into make believe I really became very interested in it myself, so I would go on and on and many a time I would be talking to myself, as Don had gone to sleep in the next room.

One or two memories of the boys being naughty at bedtime, is when they would not go to sleep and would jump up and down on the beds having high jinks. I would be in my cot, and I can remember my dad running up the stairs when the boys would dive into bed, sheets over their head and obviously frightened. Dad would have his belt in his hand. I can't remember him hitting them, but they could probably tell a different story.

My sister Betty who was eight years older than me, was probably working in service, I can't remember her being around at that time. I can remember her looking after me and taking me out with her friends, and I would tell tales if she spoke to any boys, what a little madam I must have been.

## CHAPTER THREE

Celebrations were held in 1935 for Queen Mary's jubilee. We were given Jubilee books at the school to mark this memorable occasion. I still have my rather tattered treasured book. I also have in my possession The Crowning of King George VI and Queen Elizabeth May 12th 1937. This is what it states.

'This book is presented to you by the Southampton Borough Council to commemorate a great event in the history of our Country and of the Empire. The Coronation of Their Majesties King George VI and Queen Elizabeth, whose many visits to our town as Duke and Duchess of York we remember with affection and pleasure. I hope that May 12th 1937, will long live in your memories, that you will treasure this book, and that the example set by Their Majesties will inspire you as you grow up to live, like them a life of service to your fellow men and women.

Long live the King and Queen.

Harry Chick the Mayor. 1953.'

A float was entered from the local community for the carnival. The coalman offered his truck, cleaned it and it was then ready for the great event. We gathered and clambered on, dressed in various costumes and very excited. Peter my brother aged about twelve years made a very good 'Charlie Chaplin' and Edna my friend and I dressed in one of our costumes we used in the school musical festival.

These were little black pillbox hats with a note stuck in the front and placed saucily on our heads. Our dresses were black satin tops and white skirts with various musical notes placed around, very smart. It was a very enjoyable day

In 1879 the first horse drawn tram began its journey through the main thoroughfare, and in the first week 3000 passengers popped on board.

Gradually they were phased out but the horses did not become obsolete, they functioned in many roles, pulling milk carts, bread carts, road sweeping carts and much more.

The horses would always be an attraction to children, and when they had to stay still for a period they would feed them grass or maybe feed them out of the hay-bags strapped around their necks.

At one time 200 horses were used in the network. In the early part of the 20$^{th}$ century horses began to disappear, replaced by an electric system that was to serve Southampton right up to 1949. Horses were used in the First World War. Off they would go to battle with the military and consequently many became ill or injured. If this was so they would be shipped back to Southampton to a place called 'Remount' in South Stoneham and a public house called the "Stoneham Arms" stands in its place. After this they would transfer to Oxford where they would retire into the fields and were tenderly looked after at the Blue Cross Animal sanctuary.

The trams would run on tramlines throughout main streets of the town and it was a very popular form of transport. A driver would turn a handle to operate it and always stood in the front of the vehicle to do this. A conductor would issue tickets to the passengers from his little ticket machine, accompanied by a leather bag nonchalantly slung over his shoulder, enabling him to issue and collect the fares. Stairs spiralled up to the top of the tram, mainly the people that travelled on top were smokers and it was usually dense with smoke.

There were a few open aired trams, a lovely form of travel in the summer, but a little chilly in the winter months.1949 was a sad time it was the last year of the tram service. Buses then came on the roads, and are still in existence.

From 1922 Walls- Ice-cream had tricycles with "Stop me and buy one" printed on the sides of the box like container, It contained ice cream in the form of briquettes, and frozen flavoured ice water, contained in a three cornered cardboard wrapping, were called snow-fruits today they are in the form of an ice-lolly on a stick.

The trike would travel from road to road ringing its bell, a welcome sight for the children to see. 'Elderado' was another ice-cream manufacturer. This all stopped during World War II.

After the war the era of the day-to-day, door-to-door ice cream seller was over. It was replaced by big vans usually with an Italian seller selling delicious Italian ice cream. It still continues today.

My dear father was busy working very hard in Southampton Docks, he was a fireman and one of his jobs was to stoke the fires in the big liners that visited the port. Southampton Dockland was a very active place and in the early years of the nine-teenth century it was the main workforce for Southampton men. They would maybe travel the world working on these liners if they were fortunate, or work on the liners when they docked in Southampton; it was then the task of handling cargo.

Jobs were not easily available, and many times there was no work for these men. Queuing at the Dock Gates for jobs was a daily sight. One had to take their turn, if dad wasn't working he would be queuing and Mum would be struggling with mea-gre money to feed us children. She took on extra work, clean-ing middle-class peoples' homes and bringing washing home to wash, as if she didn't have enough work to do.

I feel so sad because my brother and I used to moan and groan when we had to return the beautifully cleaned and pressed laundry housed in a big suitcase. Obviously we had to walk to the destination, which sometimes was quite a long way. We were a very proud family, and even as children we felt it was beneath us to have to do this chore. We did not appreciate all that my mother was doing to be able to put food on the table. We never ever went without good wholesome food, but luxuries were very few and far between. That came in later years.

Many times we would enjoy a trip on the floating bridge, which went backwards and forwards from Southampton to Woolston on the river Itchen, this was a great trip for us. A small amount of money was paid: adult's one-penny children halfpenny and cars would pay sixpence.

Mum would take us to the Western Shore for the day where we would sit on the stony beach and maybe have a picnic and if we were very lucky an ice cream. Sadly June 1977 we said fare-well to the historic Floating Bridge. In its place, proudly stands the Itchen Bridge.

My dad Alfred and his brothers Thomas, Frank (Wally), Ernest, Bertram, Arthur, Cecil all went to sea. He also had two sisters Louise and Mabel. Unfortunately two of the brothers, Bertram and Wally were on that fateful ship the "Titanic" which unfortunately struck an iceberg on its maiden voyage in 1912. Bertram was only 20 years old and sadly he perished.

**Bertram Terrell,**
**able bodied seaman**

**F. Terrell,**
**steward**

Bertram and Wally—Titanic Crewe—1912

Wally was fortunate, and he was saved in lifeboat number eleven, he was 26years old. It was said that Bertram was offered a space in the lifeboat after the women and children because of his age, but he was worried about his brother Wally and frantically looked for him. In the meantime Wally was lowered into the sea and Bertram was never found. Wally lost a leg and became deaf. He eventually returned to the liners and resumed his duties at sea.

This is information I have researched.

**Perished:**
Name: **Terrell, Bertram.**
Position onboard the Titanic: Able Seaman.
Place of Birth: Hampshire.
Address: 2 Trinity Cottages, St Mary's Southampton.
Age: 20 years old.
Terrell J.L: Father.
Arthur: Brother.
Cecil: Brother.
Mabel: Sister.
All class G dependants

Class G dependants received:
Dependants' relatives: 7/6d per week
Total for the family: = 22/6d.

From MANSION House,
Titanic Relief Fund Booklet, March 1913.

**Saved:**
**In lifeboat number 11**
Name: **Terrell, Frank (Wally)**
Position onboard the Titanic: Assistant Steward.
Age: 26 years old.
Address: 5 Grove Street, St Mary's, Southampton.

Other members of the family my father Alfred Terrell, Reg, and Louise were older and not eligible for any money from the relief fund.

My brother Don Terrell has in his possession Uncle Wally's seaman's discharge book, which he treasures. In the discharge book it was noted that he ceased work on the Titanic on the day it sank. The wages ceased immediately.

Obviously that is why a relief Fund was put in action to help survivors and their dependants. Uncle Wally lived for many years and was able to give information about the disaster when they made the first film of the Titanic, many years ago.

Of the many times I was in his company as a young child I never heard him speak of the Titanic. My memories of him are of a lovely man who became a baker and confectioner. He always baked lovely cakes for us and coconut pyramids were my favourite. Uncle Wally died aged about 68years 1955.

Dad met Mum on the pier at Brighton. After the First World War he was gassed in the trenches in France and was admitted to Netley Hospital Southampton and this was his home for the next two years.

He was able to go out for a day but had to wear the traditional blue uniform and white shirt and red tie. Anyone who saw soldiers in this attire knew they were patients of the hospital. My uncle Arthur accompanied him this particular day and they decided to get a train to Brighton.

Mum and her sister Dora lived in Hunstanton Norfolk. They worked in service for the wealthy and also lived in what was termed as the 'big house', usual work for young ladies who were born in that era. Usually they had one day off a month, and this, as a rule was spent visiting their parents with the exception of this particular day.

On the train they travelled on an exciting journey, not for one minute thinking they would meet the men they would eventually marry. It happened, with two sisters marrying two brothers, and after Mum and dad were married dad had to return to Netley Hospital. It was a long time of suffering, as he had to endure many operations. He had been gassed in the First World War, and his stomach was reduced to half the normal size, as such his intake of food was very small.

Netley Military Hospital—1916—Dad 3rd from left.

He enjoyed a Guinness at the local pub, and when he had the cash this is where he would go. As with most men in that era, we liked it when he had had a drink, as we would get little extras from him. He suffered all through his life and worked hard through all his pain.

My dad had a terrific sense of humour; unfortunately he died very young with cancer just reaching the age of fifty. I loved my dad. I was fifteen years of age.

In the meantime Mum managed to get a small flat let in Belmont Road Portswood where my sister Joan was born, and she would visit dad as much as she possibly could. Bassett and Swaythling were large green areas, and soon houses would be built on this ground. The first four were built in Mayfield Road and Mum and dad were offered one.

Money was short with my dad in hospital, but my Grand-dad came to the fore in Norfolk and sent her the first four weeks rent. This gave Mum a good start and this is where the rest of her children were born.

Soon, the open spaces were filled with houses, shops and schools and Mum was well established to bring up her children.

## CHAPTER FOUR

Norfolk was the county where Mum was born and lived with her sisters Ethel and Dora. Mum was the eldest. Auntie Ethel stayed in Norfolk after she was married, a very clever woman, she once made a stair carpet in tapestry. She was a lovely lady.

Grandparents—Mum—aunty Ethel—aunty Dora
(my ancestors)

The memories of Norfolk still come to the fore. Mum, Don and I would pack our cases and off we would go. It was a great adventure and we would get so excited. The train was a big attraction and we would wait anxiously at the station for the steam train to arrive. The platform also had its attractions, but it was the chocolate machine that mesmerised me. If one was lucky enough to have a penny, you would insert it in the machine and out would come a bar of nestle chocolate, it was small and thin, but oh the wonder of it all.

I can't remember having the luxury of this succulent treat myself; it was something only other people had the pleasure of. If at any time we were lucky enough to have a bar of chocolate, it would be bought at the local sweet shop where the cost would be so much cheaper. The station was magic and the chocolate machine was magical. I would be content watching the odd businessman inserting his penny, and pulling out his chocolate bar that he was then ready to enjoy on the train.

We also had our little treat whilst travelling. Tucked away in Mum's basket would be a bag of boiled sweets—humbugs, pear drops, acid drops, bull's eyes, aniseed balls and many more. Out the bag would come, twitchy hands would plunge in delving around until we eventually selected the sweet of our choice, in the mouth it was quickly popped. We would suck away trying to make it last as long as possible as it would be quite a while before we had another.

Mum purchased these boiled sweets in a little shop in St Mary's Southampton it was near the market square where they were made on the premises. A lovely aroma drifted into the nostrils, what ambience and it was all for free. (The aroma I mean).

Smoke was billowing in the station and the train had arrived. On we would clamber, looking for an empty compartment, our cases would safely be secured above our heads. The guard would blow his whistle and slowly the train would chug-chug on its journey, under the tunnel we would go and we then knew we were on our way.

Our excitement would be intense seeing the wonders of the countryside, passing through industrial towns and listening to the wheels as they click-clicked and all of us singing tunes as the locomotive sped on its way.

Much of what we did when we arrived at our destination is a blur; the beach at Hunstanton was memorable—we would sit there often and play in the sea, a tyre would be slung around our waists and we would be safe. The tyre was big and black; actually it was an inner tube from a car.

I never met my grandparents, they died before I was born in fact I never met both sides of grandparents. My sister Joan knew them, I was the youngest sibling, and unfortunately did not have this privilege.

I dearly would have loved to have had a grandma and grand-pa being the youngest of the family I did not have the luxury of this pleasure, and so no memories. A little part in my heart is sad over this. The elderly died much earlier in life than they do today. With modern medicine etc, our lives are prolonged. My ancestors on my dad's side originated from Ireland, and so again no memories.

Time leaps by and decades have passed. Joan, Reg, Bill and I made a nostalgic trip back to Norfolk, this time we motored and enjoyed every moment. We stayed in Heacham; this is where Mum lived until she went into the wide world to work.

We actually saw the cottage where she was born and we were so excited. The cottage was one of a small row and surrounded by the village green. Apparently these cottages belonged to the owner of the "Big House" as I remember Mum calling it.

My grandmother was a housemaid and grandfather was head gardener. Oh the joy on Mum's face when she would relate to us how she was allowed to go to the "big house" and play with the children. She was actually taught dancing with them when the tutor came, and very proud to tell us that she could dance the polka as good as anyone.

"The Big House" had gone, but the cottages remained with the village green in front and the old village water pump still present. A seat had been erected so we sat and reminisced, whilst gazing at Mum's cottage home.

Opposite the green was the church, snugly nestled in a picturesque scene Mum had only to walk across the road to be married. It was so tranquil. Joan and I walked up the winding pathway with such a sense of closeness to know that our ancestors worshipped here in this old church. Joan ran around and sat on every pew, as she new Mum must have sat on one of them. Mum sang soprano in the church and with the school choir.

Dad also sang at St Mary's church in Southampton. We, as descendents, love every aspect of music and many have good singing voices. One or two of my cousins have excelled in this field.

Afterwards, we visited the lavender fields, where we spent a few lovely moments. We also visited Sandringham and the Queen's residence where she stays when in Norfolk. The little church and the station where the Royal train would end its journey were quaint. We enjoyed going around the grounds and managed to visit part of their residence. There was an awful lot of history attached to our journey into Norfolk it was indeed very interesting.

# CHAPTER FIVE

My school days left a great impression on me. I lived and loved every moment of that era, trotting a short way down the road as the school was situated on the same road as our house. It was a small brick building, comparable to a cottage, nestled amongst fields. In later years the senior schools were to be built on this ground with a playground separating the two.

The little infant school I loved so much consisted of just one classroom, and it smelled of chalk and coke burning on the stove that heated the room in the winter. We would all huddle around this when we arrived. At break time we would enjoy our bottle of milk. It was a third of a pint, and the top of the bottle was fairly wide and sealed with a little cardboard lid. On this lid was a little round indentation into which we would have to press our straws to insert them.

If it was cold we would stay around the stove and I would pull out my slice of bread and butter. There were no school dinners, so the snack would help us through until dinnertime, when we would dash home to a steaming hot meal

Cod liver oil of malt was given to any undernourished child, ugh the smell of it, so fishy; if the children liked it they would lick their spoon until it shone. If there was an epidemic around (and years ago there were many outbreaks, diphtheria was one), the pupils would all line up in the cloakroom with a carton of mouth- wash and the gargling would begin.

Our desks, if I can describe these as best as I can, were a heavy plank of wood obviously polished, and resting on iron legs. This made a wooden seat to sit on, and another piece as a backrest and in front to rest our books was another flat piece of wood. The desks accommodated two pupils. Our writing materials were slates and chalk.

The teacher had a large blackboard, which was supported on an easel. With chalk in hand the teacher would write her many lessons, and we would attempt to copy.

Rags were given to clear our boards and we often had very chalky clothes. Most mothers would drape the girls in pinafores. As we progressed we were given exercise books and pencils, the teacher still taught with a blackboard and chalk.

Knitting was another achievement we mastered, and were taught with wooden needles and string. We produced dishcloths or kettle holders, all plain knitting but we were very proud to produce a practical item to take to our m

A lovely time was enjoyed in the infant school, where we were also taught country dancing. Miss Jordan, who was the headmistress, had a great passion for country dancing and we would congregate at her house. She had a beautiful lawn and this is where we would practice our various dances.

A percussion band was also formed with tambourines, triangles, kettledrums, jingle-bells, and cymbals etc. Audrey Kernan was our band- leader. Oh how I would have loved to be able to stand in front of the band with baton in hand. I played the triangle although this didn't give me much joy. I would rather have played the drums, but they were reserved for the boys, so no joy there. Even the cymbals would have suited me better, I would have been able to come in with the loud boom and crash at the end. Instead I had to tinkle along with my triangle.

Audrey Kernan was a very pretty little girl with a mass of natural golden curls. As I grew older I understood why she was picked as a band-leader, she looked so cute that when we went to the festivals, she would stand out, we won many trophies. Our age group was between five and seven years. These are a few names I can remember from my first years at school: Alan Bowers, John Stride, Billy Webber, Rex Mullins, Ken Tarr, David Gledhill, Jackie Blake, Barbara Terrell, Marie Pack, Joan Isaacs, Thelma Chalcraft, Joan Jarvis, Kathleen Sparks, Doreen Holdaway, Gladys Foster, Audrey Kernan, and Alan Eagle.

I loved every moment of my school days, I would toddle off in the mornings full off excitement and anticipation of what the day would bring. I would get there as early as possible and would play until it was time to go to class.

Games were seasonal and consisted of skipping, hopscotch, dibs, chasing, leap-frog, top and whip, marbles, conkers, hoops, kite flying, ball games flipping cigarette cards, yo-yo, and many more. So there was always lots of activity in the playgrounds.

When it was time to go to our classes a whistle would blow, and we had to stop what we were doing and stand very still like statues before lining up and marching to our classrooms. If at anytime we misbehaved we would have to put our hands on our heads.

Arms were always folded in front of us when listening to what the teachers had to say, it also helped us to sit upright there was no slouching in our classrooms.

From the little school we progressed to wooden huts, and then into the junior school, which was a big brick school, which still remains to this day. The little brick building where we were first introduced to learning was demolished for senior schools etc.

At junior school we worked very hard with our lessons and our teachers were very strict. Mr McGovern was the headmaster and it was very frightening if you had to go to his room. Above his office was another little room where a large toll bell was situated. Someone would pull ropes and the bell would ring, telling the children that it was time for school. It would toll in the mornings and if you were still at home when you heard it you would run as fast as you could to get to school before it stopped. I never had this problem. I would like to be at school early to play with my friends before lessons.

We were taught a lot in the junior school and I vividly remember the last year. The teacher was Miss Beasley and what a disciplinarian she was in training this class for scholarships. Throughout the school, classes were sectioned in A. B. and C. groups. Our class was an A class. I now realise that this was terribly wrong, as the A classes were given special tuition.

I was not an exceptionally bright pupil but I had a great hunger to learn and had to study very hard. I was pleased to be in the A class, as this was the class the children would be picked for scholarships. Fortunately my dad was always there to help me with my homework. In the glow of the evening fire we would sit together and rigorously go through what I needed to know. I was very interested in sums, and my dad also had this passion.

Early in the morning one of the first lessons was mental arithmetic, twenty sums would be fired at us, and woe beside any of us if we got one wrong. Out would come the ruler and we would stand in a line and Miss Beasley would administer a slap as hard as she could go on the palms of our hands. Oh the soreness of it all but it worked well, because at the end of term the ruler was rarely performing this horrible task.

Miss Beasley was generally very much disliked, but I didn't share this, as she would always give her time to you whenever you wanted it and would explain questions with the utmost care. "Yes, Miss Beasley," you produced a very well disciplined class and although I feared her many times, I respected her as well.

In 1937 a new junior school was built in Bassett Green and how lucky we were to be transferred to a beautiful new building. The boy's school was one side of the playground and the girl's the other side. Each classroom was airy with French windows leading out to gardens and this was the first time we were separated from the boys.

As it was coming to the end of my junior school I was obviously in the top class preparing for my scholarship, of which Miss Beasley had started to prepare us. Unfortunately she did not move with us.

I loved our new school with the new desks, one for each pupil, new pens and exercise books, inkwells and ink to dip our pens in. What joy!

The day came for the scholarship, about six pupils were picked from each school, I was very fortunate to be one of them, exams were taken at the Girls Grammar School in Hill Lane to learn and prepare for university. Results day came, and we all assembled in the hall the headmistress was on the stage, she called the names of each pupil who had passed the exam. I waited in anticipation, my name wasn't the first to be called, ah maybe I will be the next, and so on until it was the end.

My name wasn't called.

The clapping, and the beaming faces of the successful, and the congratulations given, was an awful lot to bear I was so terribly disappointed. I could not understand what had gone wrong, I had studied so hard, and I had failed, not only myself but my teacher and my parents especially my dad who had given me so much of his time. It took a long time to recover from this. I was envious of all who had passed and the uniforms they would be wearing.

This was our one and only chance of progressing. We left school at 14 years unless we were taught at grammar schools, or our parents were in the position to pay for our education. This was the end of the road where education was concerned. I had once dreamed of university, now I had to put it out of my mind.

Further education is continuous now for all age groups there are no more scholar-ships. Sixth-form colleges and universities are now open to all, and every-one, quire rightly, can now progress. Even me at the age of seventy-eight years, can take courses. And I would venture along these roads even now but unfortunately I am not now independent with my disabilities.

When I left school I studied a business course at night school, which my father paid for. It is now 1938, and Junior School had come to an end, my days at this lovely new school are over. It was then back to Mayfield Road and to the Senior School. It was indeed frightening mixing with the rest of the school children, who dwarfed the newcomers, but a new era had started and it was also exciting.

The school consisted of two large buildings, again one accommodating the boys, and one for the girls. It had a large communal hall with a stage, a clinic with a nurse in attendance, and above the classrooms another science room for laundry cooking and dressmaking. The playgrounds were large with netball pitches and areas to play shinti, a game similar to hockey, and of course there were football pitches for the boys. There were lots of grass areas and gardens; it was a lovely big spacious school, so different from the old junior school.

Different teachers taught various subjects, but we kept to the same classrooms. Smart desks were placed to sit at with inkwells and pens, and somewhere to keep our books.

French was a lesson that was new to us and I can remember Miss Brown over-pronouncing a French accent, we giggled and laughed at her (obviously behind her back) but we loved our French lessons. We all had a name to which we had to adhere.

My particular name was 'Pierre', 'Peter' in English as there was no equivalent to my name of Barbara.

As one progressed through the years and you managed to get to the top class, the French class would produce a play and this was always the highlight of any show that was produced. Parents and outsiders would come to this event, so I was keen to get to the top class so I could be a French-speaking actress and hopefully show off my skills. Such dreams, sadly for me it never happened.

I was twelve years old and after a year at my senior school. 1939 War was declared. Our lessons quickly changed to how to put on a gas mask, and what could happen in wartime. We were so frightened. My beloved French lessons came to a halt.

A mass evacuation was organised for all Southampton children to be evacuated to the country and to stay indefinitely until the war was over. Southampton was prime target for bombing.

I begged my parents to keep me with them, my brothers and sister were working and Len was in the army in Palestine the Far East. With persuasion I managed to coax my parents to let me stay.

Some of the children went to Canada some to Australia and the rest in the country districts in the U.K. I could not bear to leave home and my Mum and dad, unless I was forced. I was staying.

My education suffered, I had two years to complete, we all

left school at the age of fourteen years so from twelve years on it was indeed minimal.

Our schools were taken over by military personnel and soon our beloved classrooms were swarmed with soldiers and lorries milling about the streets, etc. Swaythling School became a barracks until the end of the war. I never returned to my favourite school that stood proudly not far from my parent's house. We soon got used to all the soldiers surrounding us, and would collect buttons and badges from them as souvenirs. The remaining children left in Southampton studied a few lessons in church halls.

Not many teachers were available as they were evacuated with the rest of the schools, so it was usually an hour each day of learning and maybe we would be taken on nature study walks, collecting leaves and wild flowers and studying wild life.

The church halls varied, St Albans Church hall was one and another was Highfield-Church—Hall. It was quite a long walk to get there. I recollect one wintertime, it was snowing hard much to our pleasure and we started our walk making a small snowball and rolled it all the way to our destination. Obviously it got larger and larger, and eventually it was very hard to move, and so we would gather round it and take turns with a push and a shove. Eventually it became bigger than us, so it had to be abandoned, and we had to get to our lessons, even though it may be only an hour's tuition.

Air raid shelters were allocated to each house and these had to be made up and assembled into the ground, this is where we would go when the air raids started. Large communal ones were dug into the ground in various areas, so if you were out, you would flee to these if necessary. Gas masks were issued, and they had to be carried with you at all times.

CHAPTER SIX

The war started September 3rd 1939. I was twelve years of age. All men at the age of eighteen years and over were called up for service in the war. It was a sad time, rationing of food began and everyone had a ration book and an identity card.

20th December 1940 London Blitz, our capital was burning it was called the Great Fire. St Paul's Cathedral survived.

1940 and soon the horrendous bombing of Southampton began. There would be a mad dash to the air-raid shelter; this became a regular occurrence, and was frightening. Throughout the nights we were dragged from our beds and down to the shelter we would flee. In the early days it was a dash for the communal shelter, which sheltered a lot of people. Mum would take flasks and food and hot-water- bottles and blankets to wrap around us, we would sit on hard benches.

Many friends were made from around the area and we entertained each other, sang lots of songs to drown the noise of the bombing and planes overhead. After the "All Clear" Don and I were able to go back to bed for a while but the men had to prepare for work, I realise now that Mum and Dad had very little sleep.

Soon our own shelters were ready for occupation. My Mum and Dad had made this little dugout quite comfortable with makeshift beds for Don and me so that we could sleep—my parents could only sit.

One horrendous time I recall is when the bombing of Southampton was really bad, Mum and I were on our own in the house. The windows and doors blew in, and the only way we could get to the shelter was through the back window. We had to jump and I was so frightened. There was an awful lot of hissing, we thought an unexploded bomb was near us; actually it was the boilers in the dairy that had been hit.

Bombs were scattered all over Southampton, and several were in the area of Bassett where we lived. It was called a stick of bombs. Lots of houses were demolished and lives lost. Friends and neighbours, who only a little while before we had been talking to, had tragically died. It was truly devastating.

My dad was out helping the injured, the incident happened as he was coming home to us. Pete was home from the sea on leave, and he had gone to the pictures with Don and a friend, Harold Martin. He ran to catch the bus home and was killed. Harold lived opposite our house it was fortunate that my brothers caught the next bus.

My dad was in the thick of it. He was returning from having a drink at the pub and was frantic, thinking that the boys would be on the bus. He helped all he could, and eventually returned to us exhausted and grateful that we were all safe.

It was only a short time before Don went into the Royal Navy Reserves in Gravesend, Kent. Pete was away on the boats in the Merchant Navy and Len was in Palestine, or maybe in

Italy or Malta. Joan was just married and lived in Sholing. So it just left Mum dad and me

After a while Mum became stressed with the air raids. My Mum's cousin who we called auntie Cis and lived at Woodgreen near Fordingbridge invited us both to stay with her until Mum felt better. I really enjoyed my stay and went to the school situated in the next village of Breamore. It was a little school with only one classroom for all age groups and it took a while to get used to it.

Another of Mum's cousins ran the village post office in Breamore and we would often visit her. It was a long walk to this school along a windy road with the river running by its side. Jack my cousin and I would take this route twice a day. As we came home to lunch, auntie Cis would have a large iron saucepan simmering on the cooking range with her special recipe of vegetable tomato soup. The aroma was very inviting and we would often have this as our lunchtime meal. It was very scrumptious and warming.

She lived in a lovely cottage situated in the middle of the village which was the main dominating feature surrounding this picturesque area. Our bedroom was tiny with a creaky sloping floor, and pretty little windows. It was reachable by some narrow winding stairs. Attached to the back of the cottage was a huge shed. It was full of logs and apples for storage, and all sorts of interesting commodities accompanied by woody smells, etc.

On a Sunday evening Uncle Bert called us into the front room, which we now call the lounge. This was where he would read the bible with his specs perched impressionably on the tip of his nose—a little man solemnly reading the scriptures. It seemed to us that he would never stop. I was completely bored, and longed to be released from this tiresome routine.

Auntie Cis was lovely but very strict, her food wasn't as varied as my Mums, breakfast was usually bread and jam and I was offered cereal but she put saccharin in the milk to sweeten it. One day I actually bit into the wretched saccharin, I never forgot the taste.

Our bread was spread with margarine—a horrible tangy taste—this was another source of food I would not eat.

My dear Mum was the same, food was on ration and e were allowed two ounces of butter a week, which unfortunately we never had from Auntie Cis. We did not complain though, we were so grateful to be with her.

When Mum was at home she used to make her own butter by continually shaking the cream from the milk. It was very creamy, and soon after a lot of hard work we had a lump of butter, which helped out with our weekly ration. Mum hated margarine and she would not give to us what she herself would not eat. Our family was blessed with a lovely Mum.

Our diet was so different to what it is today. We ate a lot of rabbit, either as a roast or delicious stews. Rabbits were not on ration so this was a good source of food, and in the country they were plentiful so it helped with the meat ration.

The countryside was a lovely place to explore and we had some interesting walks which left us with some beautiful memories of our six week stay with Auntie Cis, Uncle Burt and of course my cousin Jack. The rest of my cousins were away partaking in war service.

It was lovely to return to Southampton and my lovely dad. Mum was rested and although we missed the countryside and the peace plus all that Auntie Cis had done for us, we were still happy to be home and with each other even though the air raids continued.

## DUNKIRK

One memory that clings to my mind is seeing lots of injured French sailors lying in the roads, bandages engulfing their heads with injured limbs. Lots of lives were lost at Dunkirk, every small boat that was available helped to bring the wounded back to this island.

Our lovely school Bassett Green that I had attended as a junior was occupied as a makeshift hospital for the Dunkirk veterans. Eventually when the wounded left, the school had to be renovated and this time they chose to bring it back to its right status to a teaching school. We were able to resume our studies once again and it was then taken over temporarily as the senior school so I had my last year of schooling there. The school shelters were small buildings situated along the side of the classrooms. When the siren sounded we had to go to the shelters and would entertain each other by singing songs as loud as we possibly could to block out the noise of the air raids.

## JANUARY 1940—FOOD RATIONING BEGAN

January 1940—bacon, ham, sugar and butter.

March 1940—meat.

March 1941—treacle and syrup, jam and marmalade.

June 1942—eggs were controlled.

August 1941—extra cheese for manual workers.

November 1941—distribution of milk controlled.

December 1941—A 'points' scheme for food was introduced, together with National Dried Milk.

January 1942—rice and dried fruit added to points system.

February 1942—canned tomatoes and peas.

April 1942—cereals condensed milk on points.

June 1942—American dried egg powder on sale.

July 1942—sweets rationed.

August 1942—biscuits on points.

December 1942—extra tea for all 70 year-olds.

January 1945—whale meat for sale.

I was 14 years old and it was time for me to work. Dad paid for me to take some courses at night school, so I took the subjects of bookkeeping, shorthand and typing and enjoyed the subjects very much. I did the course with my friend Iris Vincent but unfortunately she opted out after the first year and I was silly enough to go with her. My dad was very cross, typing skills would have been so helpful especially now with using a computer.

I acquired a job in an accountant's office and progressed with bookkeeping. After about a year I became restless and wanted to join my friends who worked at Pirrelli General Cable Works. They were actually earning more money, so this was a big temptation.

I managed to get a job in the Copper Stores where again I did bookkeeping and I was very happy there for many years. I met Betty White, who worked in the wages office along with Iris Vincent and the three of us became firm friends. Betty is still my best friend.

Although the war was still in progress, there were fewer air raids in Southampton. We could distinguish our planes from the Germans by their distinct sound, 'Doodlebugs' were hitting London—there was no warning it was so very scary "Will it be Southampton next?"

My dear dad became very ill and my Mum nursed him through his terrible illness.

Unfortunately my brother Len could not get home to see his dad. He was abroad with his regiment a couple of years before the war started and so they spent a very long time apart. Dad kept asking for Len, but it was a wish that couldn't be granted even though he was awarded compassionate leave. Len was with the regular army, in the Hampshire Regiment, and at this particular time was posted in Malta.

Len—1941

The Maltese people had a horrendous time and at one particular time planes could not fly in or fly out of this brave little island. Malta was awarded the George Cross.

My dear dad died at the tender age of nearly 50 years in July 1942. It was sad that he did not have the pleasure of seeing his first grandchild. Thank goodness we had Sandra to focus on, as she was born three weeks later at the end of July. We now had to cope without the head of our family, and so it helped immensely. My dear dad I love him so. His humour, guidance and love will be missed so much—I was 15 years old.

It seems strange but I was actually enjoying life. At 16 years old I belonged to the Girls Training school where we were trained as much as possible in preparation for joining the forces when we became of age.

The year would be about 1943, and I was enjoying being a cadet. We learned to march, had lessons on aircraft recognition, basic electrical requirements like changing plugs, and lots more jobs that would help in the home while the men were away. This would take a lot of our spare time.

An advert was placed in the local paper for volunteers to work on the land and on a Sunday, coupons would be given after a certain amount of hours worked.

The farmer would mark your card at the end of a gruelling day and we would be paid one shilling an hour. It would take many weeks before we were able to get our coupons. This was more of an attraction to us than the money, although we needed this as well.

My friends and I decided we would apply and help in 'The

War Effort' we were of at the correct minimum age of 16 years. We would congregate at the Civic Centre in town where lorries or cars would take us out into the country districts where the farmers had work lined up for us. It was varied work, with mucking out the pigs and horses, haymaking, gathering fruit, cutting cabbages, and picking potatoes etc. When it was hot we would put a large cabbage leaf on our heads for protection (very ingenious)!!! The people that drove the vehicles for us were given extra petrol coupons.

Dancing was another great enjoyment. We would have to walk to the dance halls and back late at night in the blackout, fumbling our way along unless the moon was shining. Don White was our escort many times and saw us all safely home. He actually lived quite near to me. Eventually Don was called up for service and later married Betty. I was her bridesmaid.

Clothes were a big problem to us teenagers. We had our ration book for clothes, but unfortunately the coupons did not go very far and we needed dresses for dancing. We could obtain clothing coupons on the black-market. I could not afford to purchase them, however, which was a good job really as we would obviously have had to pay the penalty if we were caught.

I actually had a basic black dress and altered it a lot to make it look very different. I cut the sleeves from long to three-quarter length and then even shorter. I cut the neckline from square to round and also accessorised it many times with braids, sequins, and anything I could find. The dress looked very different and in my mind I was constantly thinking of new ideas. I loved my black dress.

Shoes were another item in short supply. Sandals were worn

a lot especially for dancing. I had a black suede pair and I was longing to own a pair white ones.

An idea came to the fore to paint them with white enamel paint. Unfortunately though, they were not completely dry before I went dancing, and what happened? Yes, they stuck to my feet! I was left with nasty sores, which hurt terribly when my feet rubbed against my shoes. My pride was also hurt. I told folk I that I was fine when I was hobbling about, just as I did when I cycled to work in the bad winter months with bare legs—mainly for the lack of stockings.

Oh the joys of being a teenager.

Mum met a lovely man; Arch Cole and we called him Pop. He looked after her well and they married in 1946. He had a grown family and I still keep in touch with Des his eldest son. Des was in the Navy, Bryan in the Army, and Connie stayed with us a while before she married. John the youngest eventually went to Australia. We all respected pop. He adored my Mum and he looked after her well and we all grew to love him.

One wonderful morning I had a fantastic surprise. Peter, my brother, had been to sea and his ship—luckily for me—had sailed to the United States. He brought me a super pair of high white wedge heel shoes, very fashionable in the States but unobtainable here.

Don and Peter—When at sea—1944

I was so excited that I wore them in bed before I got up to go to work. When I arrived at work with my lovely fashionable shoes, guess who was the envy of all her friends? Yes, me! All in sundry tried them on. I also had lots of make-up and lipsticks and chocolates that I shared with my friends my popularity soared at these times. Peter was a very generous man and I was so spoiled with my brother's kindness. My dear brother really looked after his little sister. When Pete and Don were home from sea, they each turned out their pockets and I was rewarded with their spare cash. If I needed more I had to earn it by polishing their shoes. I never went without.

Time moved forward, and in a macabre sort of way I was enjoying my teenage years—obviously the worry of the war did not affect us as much as it did our dear parents. We would go dancing not dwelling too much about the effect the war had upon us all.

Plenty of dances were held all over the place and we would often walk miles home as transport was not available and of course it was very dark with not a light on anywhere. We could not use a torch and did not even have a twinkle piercing through the houses we passed en-route. It did not worry us at all and we would laugh and tumble over situations. Usually there were several of us who lived in the same area, and so we were never alone. Don White was our knight in shining armour before he went in the forces.

Other times we were picked up from work in lorries and transported to nearby country areas where the army or air force camps were situated. They really welcomed us to their dances. There were times when we went to the local schools that the troops occupied and where again we were able to dance the night away. We were looked after very well and usually refreshments were provided which we were very grateful to receive as we could then save on our own rations. Food was always to the fore in our minds.

The American soldiers were stationed on Southampton common at one time; I think this was prior to D. Day. Gosh, when we went to their dances we were showered with sweets, chocolates, fruit and luscious cakes etc. We were able to bring some items home so that family and friends could benefit from these luxuries. We were eternally grateful as such things were either rationed or unobtainable throughout the war.

The Americans were around for about three years and had their headquarters at the Civic Centre, but I did not acquaint myself with any of them. For one thing they were hopeless at dancing, although they did bring the jitterbug dance and the jive with them. We soon caught on, kicking our legs around in high spirits—these dances were great for us and got rid of a lot of emotions.

The Yanks did have a reputation of being promiscuous; life is so totally different now. It actually changed in the sixties, before then if you became pregnant you were ushered away without anyone knowing and the babies were mostly taken away. It was a big stigma and again the worry was on the parents.

We did not have a lot of knowledge, of the do's and don'ts of life so I played safe. On the whole the Yanks were very nice, obviously not all were loud and bombastic. I mixed with them but mostly with my friends. They also spun lots of yarns of the great life they had in America, some of the girls were so vulnerable and thought they would have a great life of luxury in the U.S.A. so their eyes were only for them.

Some of us used them in a way I suppose, we were glad to accept their hospitality, but again they were grateful to us for attending their dances—many of them would never see their beloved homeland again. So it cut both ways and not all the girls were as scared as me to be alone with them on dates.

The little parcel of goodies we so gratefully accepted from them at the dances softened the blow of being chastised for returning home late, especially if the sirens had sounded. As the German planes rumbled in the skies, incendiary bombs were dropped; these would cause fires and also light up the area for bombs or mines to devastate the area.

The worry my dear Mum suffered with my brothers on the high seas, another in The Middle East and me living it up without a care in the world—Oh dear. It is lovely being a teenager, but it doesn't last long. With all the restrictions put upon us I guess we took the good times when they were available and I was selfish enough at the time to only think of myself.

D-Day—June 6 1944, a date that will forever be etched in my mind. Southampton was to be the main embarkation point on the South Coast. Giant tanks rumbled down the Avenue, transporters, jeeps and bulldozers all jockeyed for room as they disappeared behind the barbed wire compounds in the docks. The Streets were lined with army vehicles and equipment, and every nook and corner of Southampton Common was covered in large tents. As children, this had been a play area for my friends and I. Now the beautiful green grass was hardly recognisable.

Lots of houses were requisitioned in the rural areas and were soon filled with the military. Jeeps would be dashing around with the U.S.Military Police in white helmets nick -named the 'Snowdrops'. Hotels were taken over by the Military and blitzed sites were rapidly levelled for the parking of military vehicles.

It was along the Avenue, our destination was the Civic Centre forecourt in town where we were to be picked up by cars and lorries and taken to various farms in the countryside on the edge of Southampton to help the farmers.

This particular Sunday was mayhem along the Avenue. The Yanks dominated the whole area adjoining the common throwing chocolates, sweets, cigarettes and chewing gum from their lorries and tanks. We scrambled to collect them and gosh we would have some luxuries to eek out our plain sandwiches when we had our lunch! It made us so happy. A lot of chit -chat went back and forth, until finally we waved goodbye looking forward to the same procedure when we returned from the farms.

Surprise, surprise, when we did return, the Bassett Avenue was devoid of all Military personnel and vehicles, and the common looked bare. We did not know what had happened—all that remained was a stark and eerie silence. We had been looking forward to some more goodies and idle chatting, but unbeknown to us this was the beginning of the big exodus.

The Yanks were at the Docks getting ready for departure. Smoke screens bellowed upwards whenever sirens wailed a warning of air raids. Southampton was used to army personnel being around by this time, as they had been using our schools etc for barracks, but this was like an invasion and we were unaware of what was about to happen. It was all so sudden

Southwick House, just outside of Wickham, was to become the nerve centre for 'Operation Overload' in the last weeks before D-Day. On the coast at Netley, the military hospital, where my dad was a patient for two years during the First World War, prepared for casualties.

Vast ammunition stores were set up in the New Forest along with military vehicles of every shape and size hidden in the denseness of the surrounding trees.

A soldier friend of my family and me, who was stationed in GlenEyre Road in Southampton with his unit, came to see me on the day of embarkation. He was a despatch rider and was able to break ranks at the Docks and tear away to see us. He could not say anything, only a quick goodbye, and I guess he was back to his unit before he was missed. Southampton was at the centre of the biggest invasion force the world had ever seen.

The build-up in and around Southampton turned the city into a huge military camp. In the weeks before the invasion there was a tremendous military presence with British, American and Canadian troops.

The Americans began arriving in early 1942. By British standards, the American troops were prosperous, bringing with them chewing gum, chocolate, cigarettes, nylon stockings and other wartime rarities. By the beginning of 1944 there were 75,000 U.S. troops in Britain. In the final weeks before D-Day there was an estimated 1,500,000 in the country.

With the U.S troops came 13,700 wheeled and semi tracked vehicles, 4.200 tracked vehicles, and 3.500 pieces of artillery. By 1944 supplies were arriving at the rate of 750,000 tons a month.

Force B, bound for Omaha, embarked from Plymouth, Fowey, Falmouth and the Helford River. Others set sail from the Bristol Channel. Force G, destined for the assault on Gold Beach, sailed from Southampton. Force J embarked for their target, Juno Beach, from Southampton. Force L, the follow-up troops, set sail from Felixstowe, Harwich and the Thames ports. Omaha Beach left from Weymouth, Portland and Poole. Force S, who was to attack Sword Beach, set off from Portsmouth, Newhaven and Shoreham. Force U, allocated to Utah and Omaha Beaches, left from Torbay, Brixham and Salcombe.

When it came to the assault however, things did not turn out quite as had been expected. First there was the rough sea, which caused serious dislocation in important parts of the programme. The assault convoy anchored at 5.30am on June 6 some seven miles off shore. It was very choppy with a four-foot sea running.

The assault convoy anchored at 5.30am on June 6th and the men were on their troop decks by 5.45am, embarking at 6am. H hour was 7.25am. The landing craft were lowered and although the run-in was uneventful from a military point of view, most men were very seasick and all were drenched.

The beaches were invisible until the craft were some four miles off shore. A very heavy naval bombardment was in full swing and in spite of their acute seasickness and resultant depression; the troops were very much heartened by the roar of the broadsides from the six-inch guns of HMS Ajax as they passed close to her.

During the last half-mile, enemy mortar fire as well as small arms fire came down on the sea but fortunately without much effect. Some of the landing craft were lost through striking the underwater obstacles that had been dug deep into the beach.

The landing craft beached some 30yards from the edge of the sea, and the men leapt into the water. Some were up to their armpits in seawater, others up to their thighs, and immediately came under concentrated fire. Many were killed.

There were casualties too as the crafts, now lightened by the men jumping out, became water-borne again and were swept inshore by the sea over-running some of the wading soldiers. The situation was such that less seasoned or less determined troops might well have been helplessly pinned down and the whole great venture brought to a standstill.

But in spite of the demoralising effects of seasickness, in spite of the violent machine-gun and mortar fire, and in spite of the constantly rising number of casualties, the assault companies resolutely made their way on to the beach and up to the dunes.

The D-Day Normandy landings were underway.

The umbrella bombardment from Allied warships began that day as dawn broke. From left, right and centre, our guns opened up and targets ashore were pounded out of existence as the assaulting infantry sailed slowly and surely ahead to let bayonets do what ever work remained.

From sea and sky the bombardment continued, until our infantry went ashore. It was a magnificent sight. Wave upon wave of khaki-clad figures surged up the beaches overcoming any opposition in their way. Within a very short time the immediate bridgehead was ours.

In the forefront of the 'Operational Overload' landings were the troops of the Hampshire Regiment who took the time-honoured position of attacking on the right of the line.

Their orders included the capture of hamlets and villagers of Le Hamel, Asnelles-sur-mur, Tracy-sur-Mur and finally Arromanches.

The assault was planned in every detail and everything was prepared, but in the end the success of the attack depended totally on the courage and determination of the fighting force and none were more determined to win through on D-Day than the Hampshire Regiment troops.

So the Allied advance was finally underway, with the 1st Hampshire Regiment on the right of the line, and the initial assault is recorded in the official regimental history. Everyone knew how historic the occasion was, and spirits were high. The liberation of Paris was rapidly concluded on August 23rd yet this was no more the signal for the end of the war than was the liberation of Rome two months earlier.

In the east, the Red Army launched its summer offensive with a massive assault on German forces that resulted in 1.7 million troops smashing a huge hole in the 200-mile Nazi front. In just one week 38,000 German troops were killed and 116,000 taken prisoner.

With the Red Army poised outside of Warsaw and the British and American armies advancing into France, the Allies were in a strong position. Soon however, they became victims of their own success, moving so fast that they outstripped their supplies.

After the disaster at Arnham, the fierce battle of the Ardennes and the controversial bombing of Dresden, the Allied armies advanced to the banks of the Rhine and finally the symbolic crossing was achieved on March 22.

All the Germans could find to face the British forces were five tired divisions as the bulk of the best remaining troops had been moved to try and hold the Russians on the Eastern Front. Bastions of German resistance gradually fell—the Ruhr, Frankfurt, Danzig, and on April 13th the Russians entered Vienna.

The race for Berlin was on as Churchill looked uneasily at the Russian advance, insisting to Eisenhower: "We should shake hands with the Russians as far to the East as possible". At 5am on the morning of April 16, the Red Army began its offensive against Berlin as thousand of tanks crossed the River Order.

The US 9th Army was already 60 miles away but it was a Russian soldier, Sergeant Kantariya, who waved the Red Banner from the second floor of the Reichstag on April 30.

Less than a mile away, Hitler was in his bunker—a broken man. At 3.30pm he sent all those who were with him—Goebbels, Bornmann, and his personal staff-out of his room.

A few moments later they heard a single shot

The Fuehrer had shot himself in the mouth. Representatives of Admiral Karl Doenitz who succeeded Hitler surrendered unconditionally to Montgomery on Luneberg Heath on May 4.

## CHAPTER SEVEN

I enjoyed my working days at Pirelli General Cable Works. Don White was working in the Engineering department, but was not yet old enough to join the forces and hence, as previously stated, looked after us when we went dancing.

Life was good working at Pirelli I made plenty of friends, and we made the most of life through the remainder of the war years. I joined the concert party and we put on shows for the factory staff, at one time we sang on air on the B.B.C. radio station.

The programme was called 'Works Wonders'. It was broadcast at lunchtimes, for the workers all over the country to listen and to participate and helped to keep up the moral of those left on the home front. Many of these workers spent their spare time working as air-raid wardens, home guards, fire fighters and much more. They were not called up for service as they had vital jobs and were invaluable at the Home Front.

We continued to put on shows at the Pirelli General Social Club situated in Lodge Road, Southampton. Regular dances were held and the money raised from these events helped the Red Cross to send parcels to our men who had become Prisoners of War.

Through the Geneva Convention, it was agreed that the enemy was duty bound to let theses parcels get to the right resources. I volunteered to be on the committee to help raise this money, which I thought was such a worthy cause.

Little did I realise that later on in years I was to meet the love of my life that had benefited a little from these parcels.

The Guildhall at the Civic Centre was another venue for our dancing. Top bands would come from all over the country and we would dance and jitterbug the night away. We had to queue to be able to get in so we would be there as early as possible. It would be sheer devastation if we had to be turned away. Other main places were the Pier, the Pirelli club, and the Bannister Club. There were many small venues around but the Guildhall was the favourite.

In December 1943 the Bevan Boys were called up to work in the mines. One in every ten men between the ages of 18 to 25 was ordered to work on the coalface rather than the trenches because of a manpower shortage.

My darling Bill was amongst one of the first batches of men called for military service and shipped over to France with hardly any training. Before D-day and Dunkirk, reinforcements did not follow on immediately as Britain was not prepared and after a lot of fighting the poor lads were swallowed up and captured by the waiting Germans.

They were shoved into cattle-trucks and crammed in like sardines. Their destination was Germany and Poland, a journey that would take several days with no daylight. The conditions were cramped and dysentery was prevalent, so by the time they reached the camps the soldiers were in a sorry state.

Unfortunately for the next five years this was Bill's home and where he spent his 21$^{st}$ birthday. There were lots of ups and downs throughout those years in the camps in Germany and Poland. The last I believe was Poland.

Prisoners mostly worked outside of the camp in parties digging ditches, shovelling coal and burying excrement, One day whilst raiding the towns, our own aircraft actually dropped bombs on their location and the poor prisoners were showered in excrement. One can imagine the language that was shouted angrily at the planes and pilots who were completely unaware of the tragedy they had caused to their own men.

Prisoner of War Camp—1940-1945—Bill I$^{st}$ front row

The Red Cross parcels the prisoners received were very precious and did not come very often. They included warm underwear tins of food, cigarettes, toiletries, and other useful commodities. Much of these articles used to barter with the Polish people for eggs.

Chocolate, bars of soap, and warm vests were very welcomed by the Poles and these became available when the odd Red Cross Parcel got through. The main interest of the prisoners however, was how to obtain food and this dominated their daily thoughts.

On the odd occasion when he could get to perform a swap, Bill devised a little trick that worked very well. He would get out his little bundle of wood, which consisted of four blocks, each with the shape of half an egg carved into it. When he received the eggs he would insert them into the holes and fit the four pieces together so that they were unseen to the outside world. He would then tie the wood together securely and blatantly walk into the camp. Fortunately the one thing the prisoners could bring into the camp was wood for their stoves—his secret was never discovered.

On another occasion, the Poles offered the men in Bill's hut a wireless. The men were ecstatic, but there was a price to pay and they all had to go without an awful lot to be able to get it. It was decided that the men would collect any goodies that came their way via the Red Cross and parcels from home. Everyone had to agree with this project as it would enable all to get the benefit of the wireless, and after months of planning and collecting 'Operation Wireless' was all set to go.

The only way the men could get the wireless into the camp was in bits and pieces, and each part would be paid for with their treasures. 'How do we get the bits in?" was the question, and after much thought it was decided that it would have to be shipped in via the soup container, thus, soup was a no-no that day.

Eventually, after a very long time, the wireless bits were in the camp. In the meantime while this was going on, a digging operation was in progress in the hut. Floorboards were removed and a square hole big enough to take one man and a wireless, was dug from the hut into the ground. It was boarded up at the sides and bottom and the wood was taken from some of the bunks.

Bill was the carpenter, doing all of the woodwork, and in the end they had a strong secure hide-away. The floorboards were then concealed back in their rightful place. Many a time the Germans raided the huts looking for any form of digging, mainly tunnels. This hide-away was never ever found even with all the probing that had persistently gone on.

Back to the wireless, and after a very long time of struggling, going without food and with some very stressful moments, it was finally pieced together and placed in its new home. Bill often said he thought it would probably be still there. We would have liked to have the opportunity to visit the place where the camp had been but unfortunately it was never to be.

The only time anyone was allowed into the hideaway was to listen to the 9 o'clock news. With the hut guarded in case a German was nearby, each man would take his turn to listen and get to hear how the war was going. This information was then passed around the camp.

I did ask Bill if he had tried to escape, but apparently he didn't. The prisoners dug tunnels all over the camp but would just crawl to the outside and return. This sounded crazy to me. Apparently if there was an escape the whole camp was punished for days, no food and lots of other punishments.

It was explained to me that vital escapes were planned for ages and that obviously there had to be outside contacts to complete it successfully. Everyone helped. It was mostly undertaken for very important personnel such as pilots etc, so unless you were someone important it was useless thinking about it.

The Great March to the West through the winter of 1944-45, was often referred to as the 'Death March'. It was the result of Hitler's decision to prevent the liberation of the majority of the prisoners of war, whilst at the same time ensuring a good supply of hostages should circumstances demand it.

Most of the men were ill prepared for the evacuation having suffered years of poor rations and wearing clothing ill suited for the Siberian winter that enveloped them. For once, the German organisation was not up to the job and the men were forced to march long distances with little food to sustain them.

Some men had marched a thousand miles by time the spring finally came and with it, liberation by Allied Forces advancing from the West. Medical care was non-existent and frost bite and dysentery was rife. Many men fell by the wayside and were dispatched by a guard's rifle, the snow soon covering their lifeless forms.

An extract from the book "THE LAST ESCAPE" by John Nichol and Tony Rennell—the story has waited fifty-seven years to be told. Bill survived this three-month journey but unfortunately he suffered the rest of his life.

## May 8ᵗʰ 1945 VICTORY IN EUROPE.

The day of victory in Europe is not a minute old before the darkness over Southampton is pierced. Across the Dockland the sounds begin. One mighty dispassion of a ships siren blasts out the familiar dot-dot-dot-dash of V for Victory. Polish Airmen, Canadian Soldiers, U.S. Marines, and freed French Soldiers were there to celebrate with of course, our British Servicemen. Following the King's V.E night broadcast that was relayed over loudspeakers, the Mayor, Mayor's Councillor and Mrs R Stranger started the dancing on the Civic Centre forecourt. Flood- lights glared at the walls of the civic buildings. Dusk came and half of these were reversed to illuminate the dancers.

Bonfires built in the streets and on the sites of the bombed buildings, sent up a cheery glow. A sailor carrying a Union Jack on a large pole started a procession. Before it broke up after making its way round and round the Civic Centre square, and the forecourt, it was nearly half a mile long.

It was the Navy that provided other diversions, such as swimming in the fountain and performing acrobatics on top of flagpoles. Crowds who were not dancing surged backwards and forwards across the lawns and when someone started a song it was taken up by thousands of voices.

I was partaking in the celebrations, my youth still with me. I was 12 years old when war had started, and now aged 18 years I celebrated with all around me, dancing singing, hugging, kissing and generally going crazy.

Returning home sometime the next morning with, at last, not a care in the world—our world of darkness was miraculously illuminated.

Even though devastation was still around we were all lifted to great heights and it would not be long before I was to meet the love of my life. Nearly every street held parties, bunting and flags draped on houses and across the roads. Celebrations were to the fore. Hooray the War is over in Europe. Now all that was needed was victory in Japan.

Peace had returned to Europe, but at a terrible cost. During the Second World War it has been estimated that the number of people killed were:

USSR—20,000,000
POLAND—6,000,000
GERMAN—5,000,000
YUGOSLAVIA—1,600,000
ROMANIA—700,000
FRANCE—600,000
BRITAIN—400,000
HUNGARY—400,000
CZECHOSLOVAKIA- 350.000
AUSTRIA—310,000
ITALY—300,000
HOLLAND—200.000
BELGIUM—100,000
GREECE—100,000
ALBANIA—20,000
BULGARIA—17,000
FINLAND—10,000

NORWAY—10,000
DENMARK—7,000
LUXEMBUR—7,000
EUROPEAN JEWS—6,000,00

### August 15th 1945—Victory in Japan

On August 14th 1945 radio listeners in Japan were prepared for a very important announcement, and two hours after Emperor Hirohito personally announced the surrender of Japan, the country's war minister committed hara-kiri to atone for his failure.

August 15th 1945 was just a few minutes old and already the Southampton Streets had turned into one big V J. party. These were celebrations that people will never forget, and I was there.

A while earlier, at Midnight in Above Bar and all was quiet except for a couple of speeding taxis and a few GI's, lorries and private cars racing along. Then the first of thousands began shouting the news and perfect strangers shook hands and kissed each other. Searchlights took to the skies, and ships sent up coloured rockets.

Meanwhile in the town the crowds were thickening fast and within an hour Above Bar was almost impassable and draped with humanity. Lorries with shouting sailors, soldiers and civilians on their roofs, running boards and bonnets took anything up to half an hour to get through. Jeeps attained a new loading capacity. Twenty people managed to scramble on one in Above Bar. There were thirty on top of a motorcar that crawled through the crowds. Private cars ground along in bottom gear with people on their roofs and standing on back bumpers.

Early morning torrential rain doused the bonfires but not the spirits of the celebrating crowds who refused to go home and I was one of them. The Chief Constable reported the sum of told misdemeanours recorded were...four broken windows one case of drunkenness, and only one arrest

10th May 1941 to May 1945 three and a half million homes were damaged, and sixty one thousand died, half of these in London. So with all the rejoicing there was much sadness too.

Bill was a very brave man both mentally and physically to have come through five years as a P.O.W. and survived the "Long March". Eventually he was quickly shipped into England by plane where on arrival the men were escorted by a W.AAF, deloused of vermin, showered, kitted out with uniforms and offered dainty little sandwiches. They were given travelling warrants and then finally had to make their own way home.

The transition was too fast, one day they were prisoners of war and the next day they were on trains heading for their homes, very excited and also very scared. Bill did tell me of one soldier who boarded the train to Southampton. The dear man actually lived in the North but was much too nervous to return home. He had to retrace his journey in the end, how very sad that it had to happen. If only they had been rehabilitated and then sent home—at least they would have been more prepared to face what was ahead of them. It was all too much too soon.

The devastation when he arrived in Southampton Central Station was hard to bear and unfortunately he had to face the unknown alone. His father had died, his house had been bombed and his mother was living with his sister Phyllis and husband Charlie and their four young children Brian Eileen Sheila and Brenda, in a small terrace house. It was obvious there was no room for Bill even though the house was only two-doors away from his own bombed out home. He had to fit in somehow, but the situation was not ideal. Bill had not been prepared for any of this, he hadn't been told anything. There was no way his mother could have warned him of the situation, and all this could have been sorted with rehabilitation—he then would have had time to adjust and grieve.

Neighbours and friends organised parties, bunting was draped around the houses and people flocked to see him—the young boy that had gone away at the start of the war and came home a man for all to see and rejoice with. But he wanted to hide and not see anyone, and also needed the protection of his Mum if he went out of the home. He had to endure this for three months of his leave.

Extra rations were given, and instead of him being on a high he was on a permanent low. Bill would cycle to the common land, lay flat, try to relax and let the horrible feelings pass over him. He wanted to break things and it obviously unnerved him. His wish was to get back to his regiment and fellow prisoners of war he had made over the past five years. When all of the men eventually returned to base the much needed rehabilitation began, but as it was later realised, it had come much too late.

All the lads were so pleased to be with each other and they came to realise they had had the same experiences as Bill At least now they could talk and confide in one another.

Soon strict training began preparing them to fight in the far Eastern War. Fortunately V.J Day (VICTORY IN JAPAN) arrived so it did not happen. At last we could all rest in peace, no more fighting.

Everyone rejoiced now the war was over and demobbing began of all the forces. Britain gradually tried to get back to normal, and my Bill came home this time a more adjusted man.

## CHAPTER EIGHT

Bill's life was on the change, and we met at a New Years Eve Dance, 1946. As time went on we became closer and closer and we enjoyed many times together at Dances and the cinema. Bill found it a big effort to mix with my friends, and wanted only to be with me so it was a long and drawn out process to help him enjoy socialising. Eventually we got over this problem. He loved my family and was always at ease with them.

The time came when Bill and I wanted to be with each other forever and planned to be married, but what with the rationing of food and clothing coupons, houses not being rebuilt and accommodation not widely available, this was not easy for us. We aimed at our goals, saved and were constantly on the look out to rent a couple of rooms.

Excitement was all around us as were lucky to obtain some second-hand furniture, which was stored in his brothers' houses. This would enable us to save our furniture dockets for extras. Furniture was very expensive, as with anything that was mostly unobtainable.

I decided not to have an engagement ring, deciding that the furniture would take its place. We were ecstatically happy, and ready to face the world on our new adventure.

Sadly, this was not to be for long, as a blow came for my

dear Bill. He was taken ill and was diagnosed with T.B. of the lung, very scary, as there was no cure. He had been getting over a lot of his nervousness, and was so happy.

He wanted to leave me and carry on alone. I was broken hearted—our dreams were going up in flames. I am a very determined person and so in no way was I going to lose him. His life had once again been shattered and he needed me more than ever if he was going to survive. My fight with him began, but that is another story.

After a struggle with our emotions and with the help of both of our families, we named the day within a week. My sister and her friend organised food for a few friends and family, rations were given freely. Reg, my dear brother-in-law, made a cake—a chocolate sponge (as it was too short notice to gather all the ingredients for a traditional cake). It would have taken forever to collect enough rations for this but it did not matter to us, we were so happy to receive a cake at all—and it was delicious, a big treat for all who were lucky to have received some.

The wedding day was looming as we tackled a hectic three days. Many times Bill wanted to walk away from it all, even the day we booked and paid for our license. We walked up the steps of the Civic Centre and he just stood there looking very sad, and said he could not go along with it, what a situation I was in looking at this lovely man in such a state and me pushing him all the way.

I had no time left and it was my only chance, yes I understood his anguish, he was thinking of me and not of himself—a long fight lay ahead and he could die. My chance was here and although I was cruel in some respects, what could I do? I loved Bill so. I asked him, would he leave me if we were already married? Did he want to throw away my happiness as well as his own? Did he want to face his illness alone? After five years enduring the terrible ills of the Prisoner Of War Camps and fighting for his right to freedom, was this the time to throw in the towel? I knew if the answer was "yes" to all of those questions, then he wasn't the man I thought he was, and I would quietly walk away, broken hearted and never see him again. He looked at me, tears welled up in his eyes, and he looked so sad. He hugged me and we kissed. This was my lovely Bill and right then I knew he would be mine. He would not be alone; we would fight his dilemma together.

The big day arrived, and all that had been planned was in place. We were to be married at Southampton Civic Centre Registry Office, and the date was November 8th 1947. It was arranged for ten o'clock in the morning, I felt a little apprehensive—would Bill be there?

He arrived, and my dream came true—we were married.

We enjoyed a wedding breakfast at the Cowherds Inn, a gift from the best man, Norman. It was a big and wonderful surprise. What the whole wedding party knew and I didn't, was that Bill had received a telegram on the morning of our wedding day for admittance on the following Monday to the Isolation Hospital on Oakley Road, Southampton.

We at least had two days together. Monday arrived and Bill was admitted. It was the hospital that would eventually became the Chest Hospital, then the Western Hospital, and finally be demolished to make way for a Tesco Supermarket. The Health

Authority retained some of the land and a small Hospital was built which was named the Western Community Hospital, which caters for elderly patients.

He would hopefully get well, no cure was imminent—fresh air and rest, was the usual way forward. Patients were usually sent to Switzerland for a long rest in the clean fresh air, and another place where a Sanatorium was situated was Ventnor Isle of Wight. I prayed for him to live.

His Consultant Mr Beck decided to collapse his lung for complete rest. A long needle was inserted through his back in between the ribs and a thick tube and other bits and pieces pumped air around the chest. It was very antiquated equipment but it did the trick. Mr Beck was a very clever man. From then on air was pumped to surround the lung every week and it was now fully out of action and resting.

Six months passed before he was discharged from hospital but every week for the next eight years he had to return to have this treatment, as well as x-rays on the rested lung and much tender loving care. This is where I came in—and he had plenty of that.

Gradually as the years went by, less and less air was pumped around the lung until it was fully back to its normal self. It was a very painful procedure and Bill's back was pitted with small holes but he never complained. In the meantime I had managed to rent a couple of rooms at Woolston.

At last he had little nest to come home to. It may only have been a couple of small rooms, but it was heaven to us. His brothers shifted our furniture, laid lino on the floors and along with our bits and pieces, it became home. Our landlady was a dear soul and helped us so much throughout our stay. I must mention her name, Mrs Kilford, as I will never forget her.

While Bill was in Hospital, I cycled every day to see him on my way home from work. It was a very bad year with lots of ice and snow but I never missed a visit. The nurses were brilliant and a bowl of hot steaming soup waited to warm me through. The kindness shown will always be remembered.

My Mum would visit, very often giving up her rations for him and my sister Joan who worked in a hotel, often managed to chat up the chef for the odd breast of chicken. They loved Bill, as did a lot of people.

Bill's Mum—a wonderful lady—was so devastated. She had gone through so much worry with her young son, who at one time was reported missing and then finally ended up in a prisoner of war camp. She did not know of his long march across Poland into Germany, she only learned this when he arrived home.

There was no communication at all, in that terrible time, he was three months on the move and hence Bill did not learn of his father's death. Nowadays his terrible disease can be controlled by antibiotics and other drugs, but at the time for Bill it presented yet another fight.

Mum was, as I said before, a lovely lady and was strong for her son. She would visit Bill with goodies and eventually lived with us for 20 years.

Food was still rationed and Bill needed extra nutrition. Both families were very supportive and we all willed him to live in our own little way. My brothers liked to help as much as possible; Don and Peter still sailed on the ships in the merchant navy and were able to bring home goodies. Len was demobbed from the regular army and was working at Ranks flour Mills.

Bill eventually returned to me from hospital and we enjoyed every moment in our little home, and it was lovely to be together at last.

Mrs Kilford really spoiled us and would insist on cooking Sunday Roast. "Rest in bed" she would say and up would come the Sunday papers, which she had bought herself. Mr Kilford insisted we should read them first. At that time we could not afford to buy papers, we survived on Bills pension. Just before lunch was ready she trotted up the stairs with a roast potato on a fork, what luxury! Bill was overwhelmed. Lunch was then announced and we would trot into our room where the table was laid and a lovely meal was enjoyed. As you might guess we enjoyed our Sundays.

The small things in life were wonderful to us.

My sister Joan and Reg moved to the village of Stickland near Blandford, where they purchased a business consisting of a village store and a Bakery. It was the Bakery that had attracted Reg.

They thought the air in Dorset would be good for Bill, and so looked out for a place for us to live. We were very excited when a cottage was found in the next village to theirs named Houghton. The cottage was very tiny but would suit our needs.

It had a well in the garden and no drainage. Whilst this was certainly a novelty, it was also a chore when we had to draw every drop of water for washing, drinking and everything that one needed water for. We were young though, and soon got used to this.

Joan and Me—1948

Visitors loved the novelty, it had great advantages—the water was so pure and ice cold. There was no sink in the kitchen so Bill installed one and made a soak–away. An Elsa toilet, which had to be used with chemicals, was at the rear of the back garden.

The house consisted of three rooms downstairs and two upstairs. There was a large hallway leading to the rickety stairs, and the front door actually led into the main living room. It was strange that we never knew the reason why.

The floors consisted of stone slabs with matting laid over the middle whilst the surrounding areas were finished with red cardinal polish. A lot of work was involved in polishing these slabs every day, but it looked very nice.

The room had a big fireplace where logs collected from the woods were burned. The kitchen was adequate for our needs, a bread oven had been built in one of the walls and it indicated how thick the walls were. We never used the oven but we left it as a feature.

We actually cooked on primus stoves in the early days and then managed to save some pennies for a baby belling—a cooker with one hotplate. It was surprising what we managed to cook on that little cooker especially as we had constant visitors.

Washdays were a little bit of a chore. Clothes were boiled in a bucket on the primus stove that one would normally use for camping, but we had no choice. So much water was needed on washdays and it eventually had to be thrown away as we had no drainage. Despite this, we managed and were so happy. It was our little abode and we were with each other. Bill was slowly recovering.

The laundry could have been washed at the local laundry in the next village but unfortunately we were not able to afford this luxury, but we didn't care, it did not matter to us.

Bill's Mum came to live with us. She was a lovely lady and stayed for the next twenty years. She would have been about seventy years old then, but was very young in mind and very active. Dear Mum had returned to her native Dorset where she was born and would often visit Dorchester and her relatives. As a young lady she actually worked as a cook-housekeeper for Thomas Hardy the famous author.

Our cottage had small picturesque windows. The front garden was laid with grass and surrounded by shrubs, leading down to the road by steps. Opposite was a quaint little church, nestling in surrounding trees and the backdrop of small hills. Farmhouse cows and cottages etc completed the picture of this sleepy little hamlet.

The back garden was grass-covered and a large area by the side was the vegetable patch where Bill grew a variety of organic vegetables. When visitors came from Southampton we were able to supply them with some lovely fresh fruit and veg. A large shed was situated at the back of the garden where logs and many other items were stored. Behind this was a beautiful meadow where cows grazed often poking their heads over the wire fence to see what was going on, Very inquisitive animals, we found out.

As one passed along the lane we would often meet the rabbit catcher, a little man heavily bearded with a mass of curly hair. This is the chap who supplied us with our rabbits—our main source of food. I would make mouth-watering stews, and roast rabbit—absolutely delicious.

Further along the lane were more meadows where cows grazed and one would come across the odd little cottage. This is where the hamlet ended. There was no through road so one can understand why it was such a sleepy little village.

Early in the morning or in the twilight of the evening, we would venture out to gather mushrooms and at times would be chased by the young heifers (cows). Gradually they would descend down the hills to see what was going on and if one started to gallop, the others would follow. We would run and be laughing at the same time. On one occasion this happened when we took Laddie our dog with us. An agitated cow followed us, bellowing menacingly. I ran as fast as I could. The farmer Mr Martin came out to greet us as we neared the bottom of the meadow—he was beaming. "Don't worry, stay calm", was his remark. "The cow has just had her calf taken away and thinks the dog is her calf" It all ended very well and became a good talking point.

Farmer Martin supplied the milk to both ours, and the adjoining villages. We lived nearly opposite the farm and would take our jug daily to be filled with thick creamy milk, which played a big part in Bill's recovery.

Mum and pop visited often but they would stay at the Busy Bee Store with Joan and Reg as they had more room. They loved Dorset.

Further along the lane in the direction of the next village, Strickland, were the beds of luscious watercress that grew in the natural spring water. These also supplied the villagers with work. We were living in an agricultural area where corn and wheat and vegetables grew and animals grazed. Many times we helped the farmers with haymaking and were rewarded with jugs of cider. A winding stream ran all the way into Strickland, and it made a pretty little walk from our hamlet.

Back to our little cottage, the hallway with the stairs leading from it also had a stone flag floor. Bill made and put up a couple of shelves for the purpose of storing bottles of tomatoes. He produced lots of tomatoes, which would be freshly picked and bottled in kilner–jars, and the jars would then be placed in a large saucepan and steamed.

We had the luxury of tomatoes all winter. One must remember that food wasn't frozen in those days. We had no freezers, fridges, washing machines or vacuum cleaners—unless of course, one was relatively well off. Fruit and vegetables were obtainable only in seasons. Food was still rationed and would be supplemented by growing and collecting mushrooms in the fields and berries from the hedgerows, etc.

We would gather wild flowers—bluebells from the woods, cowslips in the meadows, and primroses along the banks etc. So our home was always adorned with pretty flowers and sweet fragrances. On the odd occasion we would walk to 'Bullbarrow', which was a beauty spot on a very high point in the surrounding area. It was a long walk, and one that we usually undertook when the bluebells were in bloom. We mainly made the visit however, when Reg took us in the van. Joan would prepare a picnic and we would lie on the hills and enjoy the magnificent views around us.

Rabbits were in abundance and would scamper over the hills bobbing their white tails. Chickens ran around freely in peoples' gardens and often ventured in the lanes. Their main function was to produce eggs and we always had plenty of fresh ones. It was very rare that one had chicken for a meal; this was indeed a luxury unless of course you had your own run in the garden. We mainly consumed chickens at Christmas.

The chickens were free-range and very succulent; fed mainly on corn and cooked potato peelings etc. One would hear the cockerel crowing in the early mornings, a lovely country sound.

The rest of the house had two bedrooms leading from the windy creaking stairs, but we only had furniture for one bedroom. Bill made a super little dressing table out of orange boxes and I draped it with pretty material. The top was made into a kidney shape and the whole thing was displayed in the corner of the room. It was very practical, as when the curtains were pulled, the shelves were displayed revealing the clothes we had packed in. A mirror was placed on the top so this was quite nice for the visitors' room. Utility furniture was still on dockets, so one had to scurry around auction sales for what was needed and what one could afford. Bill's War Pension was our sole income, there was no help with extra benefits in those days, but we economized and survived without any form of debt. Our enjoyment was our peaceful life and each other, even though money was in short supply.

We would often walk into Strickland to visit Joan and Reg. Eventually Bill helped Reg with his bookwork and I helped in the shop, in return for which we would have a good cooked meal that Joan prepared. So although luxuries were in short supply, we did not go without the good things in life—food.

From the time I met my darling, the one thing that was most dominant on his mind was the promise he had made to himself after returning home from the war that he would never starve again. He would steal food rather than go without. Fortunately this never happened, as I made sure that Bill would have the best I could possibly give. Luckily he enjoyed his food and had a good appetite which certainly helped him on the way to getting better.

Bill would often use his bicycle and ride to the shop. Our dog called 'Laddie' a cross between an Old English sheepdog and an Airedale loved to accompany Bill on these trips. As a puppy he would ride on the front of the bike in a wooden tomato box and loved every moment of his new form of travel. It was quite laughable as he grew, as he would jump up and just about manage to perch himself into it. It amused passers by a lot, and was a regular village sight. The time came when obviously it was impossible for him to sit in it anymore, but this did not deter him. When the time came for Bill to set off, Laddie would be there waiting for him to alight the bike, and would run as fast as he could over the hills, chasing the odd rabbit or two and disturbing their play. The rabbits were too cute for Laddie. After his failed escapade he would end up at the shop before Bill, it was good fun all round, our lovely dog was always triumphantly first.

After Laddie came Max who sadly had to be put to sleep. Another dog followed him, a Red setter we named Kim. He was so friendly this lovely puppy with gangly legs—so mischievous and full of excitement. He grew and grew and we had this large beautiful red dog.

After about a year Kim had to leave us. He never calmed down even though he was taken out on lots of rambles. Bill would get on his bike and Kim would run by the side of him along the lanes. He would cycle as fast as he possibly could and the dog would just lope along never ever tiring, but his master would be exhausted. Sadly, for Kim's sake, we had to let him go. A farmer was very interested in him and he had a new home as a gundog. We found out later that Kim was very happy in his new natural role. "No more dogs" Bill vowed, as I would get so upset when they were no longer around. I pined so much.

Many friends and relatives visited us, and would often stay for a holiday. They too enjoyed the tranquillity of our village life. With the aftermath of the war this was obviously heaven sent, and the children loved to tumble in the hay. Eileen would be about eight years old at this time and enjoyed a holiday with us but Sheila was very shy. Bill would try to persuade her to come, but she would not relent. Brenda was too young to stay, but Brian was much older and would come and visit on his own. These were the children of Bill's sister Phyllis. Bills brother's boys, Dereck and Ken, also enjoyed it very much, and David, the son of Bill's brother Harold, would particularly enjoy the dogs—especially Max. Then there was Alan, son of Ron, Bill's eldest brother.

Eileen and Sandra (my sister Joan's daughter) loved to gather cowslips, make friends with the animals and generally explore the countryside, gathering flowers. Most of all they scrambled amongst each other to pull the water from the well. Many times a visit would be made to Strickland and into the bakery they would go to watch Reg make the bread and cakes. Sometimes he would let them participate.

My brothers would stay with Joan and Reg at the shop. It wasn't far for them to pop to see us. Betty and Don our good friends from Southampton often visited too and we had wonderful fun together including many walks and rambles gathering food and enjoying the stream that ran from Houghton into Strickland. Twigs would be gathered and down the stream they would float. This we called our "boat race"—simple joys added to a simple life.

Reg was very good at organising trips to the beach. Out would come the old bread van and he would take out all the shelves to put some sort of seating in. Primus stoves and cooking utensils were also included. Joan would pack all the food and Sandra, Yvonne, Andrew, Bill and I would all pile in. I often think of how we all managed as it was only a small van. Andrew and Yvonne were small children and Sandra was only a little older so I think they sat on the floor or on our laps. Reg was only really allowed to use the van for business purposes, thus had to produce dockets to obtain the red petrol. Petrol was still rationed after the war and only so much was allowed for cars. Reg always took some bread with him just in case a policeman stopped him, as it would give the impression that he was delivering. If a policeman was about, we would all duck down in the van.

Fortunately he was never stopped.

Eventually we would get to the beach, and all would pile out. On the way home we would pull in at a country area and out would come the primus stoves. Reg and Bill would cook bacon and eggs, other times Joan would pack a picnic basket. On occasion, various people from the village would ask Reg to organise a bus and we would have great times. Reg always took the primus stoves and kettle and would brew tea for all of us with Bill's help.

Not many people had cars—they were a luxury and if they did, they would have to use their petrol ration sparingly.

# CHAPTER NINE

After several years we managed to rent a council house in the Village of Strickland. It was a big double fronted house and had just been newly built. We missed our little cottage and had sad moments when we were leaving, but it was lovely to have running water and a lovely bathroom.

Bill was still able to grow his vegetables as we were blessed with a long garden. The front of the house was laid out as two lawns one either side of a long sloping path and the grass was cut with a rip hook. There was quite an art to this and one could get quite skilled after practice.

Betty and Don were the first to visit, this time with their baby daughter Teresa; she did her first steps on our lawn.

One memory from living in Strickland was the Queen's Coronation in 1953. I decorated our house and made a big crown that was displayed in the front porch. Bill, Freddie Waterman and Geoff Oxendale, the local schoolteacher, built a dragon for the village fete and carnival. It was a massive thing and was housed in Fred's garden. His house was only two-doors away from ours.

It was a great celebration for a small village and it ended with a pig being roasted in a field for all to partake and a football match was organised between the men and woman. It was hilarious! The men had to wear women's garments whilst the ladies could wear shorts and the referee had a huge alarm clock strapped to his wrist. It was a rough and tumble match and I can remember picking up the ball and running like blazes, throwing the ball into the goalmouth. Naturally, the women won and we were then carted in wheelbarrows to the local pub where we were presented with the cup.

The village hall was used for many events—weddings, parties, dances, pantomimes, meetings and flower shows etc. The villagers in nearby areas would come to our dances and we would go to theirs. All would have great fun.

The British Legion also had a hall in the village and Bill made a skittle alley for them. People would come from miles around and enjoy a game. When it was a big game they played to win a pig—so it was a big attraction.

The village pub was also another attraction for the farm workers as they finished their hard days work. Many a night we would enjoy their company as they gathered and sang their country songs and naturally we would all join in. We would also play shove-halfpenny and darts—some wonderful uplifting times were enjoyed.

Maggie Stone was a cockney and had come to the village from London when the war was raging. When the war ended, she stayed on and worked as the cook for the village school. At one time I worked with her but could only work a few hours, as it would mean Bill's war pension would be reduced. It was hard work in the kitchens. All the vegetables were fresh and often came from the school gardens—the mounds of potatoes, cabbage, carrots, and swede etc, were there to peel every day.

Fruit such as gooseberries and blackcurrants were gathered and what a mammoth task topping and tailing them was! Pastry was freshly made. The children ate good wholesome food. Whenever Maggie was around there was always lots of fun and laughter, quite a character. She has since died.

Liz Herbert was my village friend and I worked on and off with her at the Busy Bee Store. This was Reg's Shop. She was a very nice girl with a real Dorset accent. At one time I was dragged along to be the village Brown Owl to the local children and Liz was always there to help.

Una, Reg's daughter from his first marriage, came to live with Reg and Joan. She helped in the bakery and the shop and we became firm friends.

Bill was well on the road to recovery and after eight years he was pronounced fit for work. No more weekly visits to Dorchester Hospital—what a welcome relief for him. The time came for rehabilitation and off he went to Kent for about six weeks and then onto Clerks College Southampton for a bookkeeping course. He was advised not return to his old trade, as a carpenter and joiner. I missed him so, as we had never been parted.

We had been together about six years when we found out that pregnancy was eluding me. I sought help, and as a result had to be admitted to Dorchester Hospital for an operation. I was given a year to fall pregnant.

Lo and behold, after eight years together, a great joy was to enter our lives. I found out that I was pregnant with Lesley. I was over the moon and Bill was ecstatic. Unfortunately no other babies came our way, but we were blessed with a baby girl—which we had both wished for.

I stayed in Strickland while Bill was at college in Southampton. Fortunately he was able to stay with my Mum, so I knew he would be well looked after. He came to see me at weekends, which would take a half-day of travel. The journey would start from Southampton to Salisbury by Hants and Dorset bus, and then on another bus to Bland ford, Dorset. When at Bland ford there was usually a wait until the small local bus arrived—then this would slowly wend its way to the village of Strickland.

The driver who was named Errol sat with his cap perched on his head and a pipe in his mouth. His actions were very slow and now and then he would stop the vehicle, get out and deliver the odd goods to various cottages along the way. Sometimes he would even stop and have a chat. The old bus would eventually arrive in Strickland and stop just outside of the Busy Bee Store—the end of the journey for us. It would eventually meander on to various other villages.

There was another driver Stan who drove the bus a little faster that Errol, but was still slow. When we lived in the village of Houghton, Stan would often get out of the bus and knock on the door for Bill sometimes. Bill would be running out with a slice of toast in his hand while the passengers sat and looked on. It was so laid back—such a serene life.

That journey from Southampton that took half of the day in the forties and fifties will only take just over an hour today in a car with part motorway travelling.

As my pregnancy was progressing, I found myself longing to join Bill in Southampton and so I moved to the city. I was happy to be with Bill and also back under the wing of my Mum. I decided to have my baby here, as eventually when Bill was working, I would be moving back to Southampton.

My baby was born in the Maternity unit, a beautiful baby girl. We named her Lesley Ann, and she weighed eight and three-quarter pounds, we were all so happy. My Mum, my stepfather, Bill and Bill's Mum came to the house as soon as I arrived home to join in the jollifications. I had stayed in the unit for ten days, where the only people allowed to visit were the dads. Time was restricted and no one was allowed at the birth or while I was in labour.

I enjoyed my stay with Mum and Pop and they loved having a baby around. My Mum would love to bath and dress Lesley in the mornings, play with her and cuddle her until eventually into her pram she would go and out into the garden to get plenty of fresh air—whatever the weather. She would be tucked up warmly and there she would stay; only to be brought in between feeds. Obviously I would be proudly taking her out for walks.

On one of these occasions I met Eileen Bessant at the baby clinic and we became firm friends. Our babies grew up together in their pre-school years. Occasionally when we returned from the clinic Eileen would come in for a cup of tea and Mum would be so happy, as she had two babies to fuss over.

As time moved on we were ready to settle in our own home with our baby. Luckily we were able to exchange our house in Dorset for one in Freemantle, Southampton. It was not where we would have chosen to live but we had no choice. The house needed a lot of work doing to it before it would suitable for me to move in with my baby, so it was painted and decorated throughout in Bill's spare time.

The time came for us to leave. Mum was so upset—she so loved Bill our baby and I living with her and Pop. We saw her often though. I would walk to her house with Lesley in the pram each week and we would stay for lunch. The walk was quite long but also rewarding—pushing the pram whilst cooing and singing to Lesley.

Mum would visit us and often Bill's Mum would join her and it would enable us to visit the cinema in the evening. Bill had started work at Swifts Wholesale meat Company as an accounts clerk and as time went on he became 'under manager' and sold the meat to the butchers. As you can imagine he had early starts, but he loved his job and stayed for many years.

In the meantime I enjoyed looking after Lesley and soon she was blossoming from a baby into a dear little girl. Bill's Mum came back to live with Lesley and us was a great source of enjoyment to her. Our little girl could do no wrong in Mum's eyes.

We often visited Charlie and Vera on the Isle of Wight, who by this time, were parents to two children—Margaret and John. Lesley loved these trips. She adored the Island and all of its beaches. We would often visit with the family. Charlie had a car so it was easy to travel about.

Lesley was younger than Margaret and loved to be with her when she played her Beatles music and was very interested in her style of clothes. The Isle-of Wight is still a favourite of ours. Sadly Vera and Charlie have since died.

A new garage was built in Winchester road, named 'Seawards'. A friend asked if I would join her serving petrol. Two or three girls would be serving at a time, as it was a busy petrol station. I discussed it with Bill and it was decided that I could work two or three evenings a week from 6pm—9pm as well as the odd Saturday or Sunday morning. Bill would be home so there would be no worry.

Seawards decided to sell Jet Petrol at greatly reduced prices and we were very busy. There was always a long queue for us to serve.

The girls I worked with were great and I enjoyed my job. Their names were: Doris Drysdal, Gregg, Doris Longman, Norah Hatfield, Jean Selby, Jean Penny, Mona, the twins—Yvonne and Yvette, and many more. Sadly Doris Drysdal and Gregg, Doris Longman, Norah Hatfield, Mona and Yvette have since died. I still keep in touch with Jean Penny and Jean Selby. Jean has remarried and her name is now Russel-Penny.

Lesley was growing and we wanted to move house before she started school. Luck was with us, as we managed to exchange our house with another in Hollybrook on a lovely little estate surrounded by trees. The house was about 2 years old. Lesley was now four and we were able to enrol her at Hollybrook School, enabling her to have a placement when she became five years old.

After about seven years at Seawards I became restless and yearned to get back to clerical work. Lesley was twelve years old and had moved to a Senior School.

I was able to resume full time work and managed to get a job as a clerk cashier at the Automobile Association. It was strange at first. I think the year was 1967 and computer work was coming to the fore. Although we did not have one in the office a lot of computer work would come from head office in Basingstoke, and it meant a lot of coding out for us.

Credit and debit cards were not around and so payment for the member's fees came mainly in the form of cheques and cash that had to be counted and banked each day. I enjoyed my days at the A.A. I worked with two young girls and a supervisor in the office. The girls brought a ray of light to the staff and were fun to be with.

I was there for just a year when unfortunately the offices were being transferred to Basingstoke. Computers were now taking over. Transfers were offered but obviously it was too far too travel so most of us sought new jobs. The firm had its natural wastages.

Before I left, Bill's Mum died at the age of 94. It was so sudden. I had to leave work that day, uncertain as to what had happened. My neighbour John Wilson collected me.

On arriving home, Bill was waiting for me to tell me the sad news. I was shocked and broken- hearted, I loved her so much. She was my friend and confidant and we would all miss her as she was always there for us all. Mum never suffered any illness the 20 years she lived with us.

Lesley was home and Iris Wilson, my friend and neighbour, came to Mum's side when Lesley told her she was unwell. Bill arrived home just before she died. It was lovely that Mum died that way, but unfortunately it took me a long time to come to terms with it.

I applied for another job, this time it was in the personnel dept of Dock House and after several interviews I was lucky enough to get the position. Unfortunately I hadn't been there long when I had to go into hospital with a suspected appendicitis. My new work colleagues were lovely and I had lots of visits and goodwill wishes.

Time went on and then I was ill again, this was not at all like me. I was 40 years old and I had a nervous breakdown. I was terribly unwell, again. I had good wishes from Dock House staff, they said to stay off work as long as it took to get well, my job would be waiting for me.

They were so good, but I had to let go and so my notice was given. At that time I could not care for anything, I was lifeless. I couldn't eat and lost a lot of weight. All I wanted to do was hide myself away and not speak to anyone. It was a terrible strain for Bill and Lesley to bear, but they were wonderful. Unfortunately at that time I did not appreciate it, but now I will never forget.

Doctor Ramsey called often and after a while when there was no improvement and he could see me deteriorating, he suggested I should go to a psychiatric hospital to get well. I pleaded with Bill to let me stay home.

I stayed, but gradually it got worse. It was an effort to get out of bed. It was an awful time, my legs felt as though they were full of worms and the butterflies in my stomach did not stop fluttering, what was happening to me? I was frightened of everything and every-one around me.

Eventually I had to see a psychiatrist and that was the turning point. Apparently I was suffering from guilt over not being with Mum when she needed me the most, and the fact that she had died without me saying goodbye and thanking her for all she had done.

I started very slowly to get better, but it took a long time. I was beginning to come to terms with my guilt but to this day it is still at the back of my mind. The doctor and psychiatrist said that Mum would have died anyway and I could not have done anything about it—but it was hard to accept. Only time helped.

After about a year I tried to get back to work. I applied for a job in the catering department at the General Hospital. I thought the interview would be one step forward and then I could apply again. Unfortunately for me at the time I got the position, it may be strange to say this, but I didn't want the job. I new I wasn't fully well.

Bill was so pleased that I had made the attempt, it was the first time I had gone out alone. This was very hard for me—each step I took, I wanted to just run back home to be safe. He was so elated that I felt I couldn't disappoint him—he had endured so much. So I took the job.

It was hell. Bill would meet me from work and I would plead with him not to go in the next day. He was so good and said, "Lets try one more day." It was so hard for me. I visited my G.P regularly and between the two I gradually got well. I never want to experience this terrible illness again. I was still to have a long struggle ahead, but eventually I would get well.

Bill became redundant from his job after twenty odd years service and was devastated. What was he to do? Fortunately another wholesale meat company soon claimed him, but this would not be for long as they would close down, the same as Swifts. Supermarkets were shooting up all over and were selling pre-packed meat; soon small butcher shops were closing for good.

John Ramshaw (the district catering manager) heard of Bill's plight through John Wane, my boss. An appointment was made for the two to meet and he asked Bill if he would like to set up buying meat for the N.H.S. It would entail buying bulk meat for all the hospitals in the region. A butchery department would be set up at Knowle Hospital where the meat would be delivered and cut and sent to the various hospitals.

This was a new position and Bill had to do the initial work, as John Ramshaw wasn't trained in this field. He offered Bill an office and a desk and that was that. Obviously Bill had connections (including some at Smithfield Market) from his previous job in the wholesale meat business, and he succeeded. Only the best meat was purchased at competitive prices and he proved to be an exceptional and very popular buyer.

Bill became the only Meat Buyer in the N.H.S. Prior to this meat was usually purchased from the local wholesalers for individual hospitals. It was a great success and I was very proud when I was told that Bill had saved the treasurer a huge amount of money. He loved his job, and did plenty of travelling to various hospitals where he made lots of friends. Of all the Catering Managers, his favourite was Patricia O'Neil of Moorgreen Hospital. I still keep in touch with Pat who retired a long time ago.

It was great with Bill working at the hospital, as we were able to go to work together, no more walking for me, especially when the weather was bad.

A new department was added to the hospital named the Neurological Unit. I still worked in the catering dept and saw many changes occur, especially the fields surrounding it. The old maternity unit was in the distance, and below the Neuro Unit, a new dining room and kitchens were built—a venue for staff to eat. A long covered walkway was attached to each hospital and members of staff were able to have their meals in either dining area.

The local pig farmer collected all of the food waste from the General Hospital on a daily basis. This is where I actually commenced my job. I worked happily at the hospital for the next twenty years.

## CHAPTER TEN

Lesley started her career at Tyrell and Green, a local store in Southampton as an apprentice-hairdresser, which included courses on hair colouring and manicuring.

She met Graham and soon he dutifully asked if they could be wed. We considered all aspects and explained the hard work that life would throw at them. They managed to get a mortgage on a very nice new flat, so Lesley needed to work full time and run a home as well. She convinced us that she could. They were in love, and so we gave them our blessings. We put all our energies into arranging a beautiful wedding, and on September 19th 1974, they married—both at the age of 20 years. Lesley made a beautiful bride and her dad was so very proud to walk her down the aisle.

She had four bridesmaids: Ann, Teresa, Julie, and Louise. Rob was the best man. Within a couple of years they had two boys Ryan and Elliott.

Over the years we somehow managed to unofficially adopt Louise when she lost her dad. She had no grandparents and so we stood in. Louise is the same age as Ryan who is currently 29 years and Elliott 27 years.

I continued to work at the hospital and was eventually transferred to the Old General for a while where I worked alongside Ann Cooper who was secretary to John Wane. It was quiet where we worked but we had great fun.

I enrolled in a car maintenance class within the hospital that enabled staff to get a little knowledge of their cars. I enjoyed the course and on the final day I undertook the job of giving Bill's car a complete service, obviously under the scrutinized eye of the instructor. My dear Bill was a little apprehensive when he first drove off but all was well and I was very pleased with myself.

Another time I took a course at an evening class for carpentry. This was a hoot as far as I was concerned! I just could not saw a straight line on a piece of wood however I did manage to complete a bevel edged tray with a little help from the tutor. After this he suggested that I did some whittling as he thought I had a creative streak and that this would suit me. Actually it was a great idea.

Some twigs of wood were what I needed to work on and the ewe tree was to be the source. Ewes mainly grow in churchyards. The tutor kindly gave me my first twigs and I was elated and excited. It would be wonderful if I was able to produce something interesting although it was a challenge. One needed to study the twig, to see if it resembled something, or could be carved and created into a shape that resembled something.

I had my carving tools and started to whittle, trying to follow the shape of the piece of ewe. It was time consuming but very relaxing. I was really enjoying my new task. Eventually something that looked like a giraffe was emerging. I was 'over the moon'. The markings were great. Ewe is a very interesting wood with the many grains running through, different colours of browns and creams.

Disaster struck, but not for long, I turned it around and before long a fish emerged, the fins were there, and I could see the gills and eyes all embedded in the wood. Eventually the carving was finished.

Rubbing down was the next step, this took a long time, but eventually it was finished. I intended to take this up as a hobby but I had to find the bits of wood and twigs and these weren't easily accessible to me. It is something I still want to pursue.

I made many friends at the hospital including Yvonne Moore who has lived in Canada for the past 29 years. The week she left, Southampton football club were celebrating their Cup Final victory. The year was 1976 and Ryan our grandson was three months old.

My dear stepfather died of cancer. I was with him and able to comfort him in his last moments. I held his hand as he sadly passed away in hospital.

My Mum was beginning to get very frail with many problems and as she worsened, more help was needed. I had chatted to Bill about her coming to live with us. We could convert the bedroom into a small bed-sit and Mum could stay there through the day while we worked. I would ask Iris my neighbour if she could pop in and give her lunch that we would have ready.

It wasn't the most ideal of situations but at least I could be home with Mum when I finished work. Peter had been staying with her through the days as he worked nights and I sat through the evenings and some of the nights. It was a plan that would also relieve Peter of the running around that he did for both her, and Pop. He was wonderful to them both.

Unfortunately though, our plans could not be put into action as on Mother's Day 1976, after spending the day with us my lovely Mum died that night of thrombosis in the leg.

The wonderful memories she has left are to me outstanding and endearing. Thank you Mum for all you did for me and my family, and thank you Pop for looking after Mum. We loved you both so much.

Back to the General Hospital the nursing staff would pass through the dining room and show their keys, no money was exchanged as the nurses were under the wing of a matron—it was a way to make sure a meal was taken regularly. Payment was taken from their salary. Staff nurses, sisters, and matrons etc all had their separate rooms to eat and were waited on by the catering staff.

Changes were being made however, and soon everyone would be eating in one dining area. Tills were established—and this is where I came in. I would take money as staff passed through with their meals and the rest of my day was spent doing clerical work. I shared the office with Lena Noke the supervisor.

Eventually, after finally getting over my illness, I began to enjoy my work. Lena gave me the encouragement I needed. Many friends were made amongst the catering staff. I am still in touch with Joan Adams, one of the staff members at that time at that time, which is nice in our twilight years.

Lots of functions were held and many times I got involved with these—it was fun. Each year, the catering staff enjoyed a party where the medical staff would wait on them—it was certainly a fun time especially as doctors and surgeons would be wiping their brows after a bout of washing up or sweeping the floors and collecting all the beer and wine glasses. It was greatly appreciated.

The South Academic Wing emerged for teaching. It had large medical libraries, and a new dining room and kitchen. This very large room became the new area for staff eating -the Neuro dining facilities were disbanded.

Years on another building began to emerge and a new wing appeared—the East-Wing. This was joined by the accident and emergency department, which was transferred from the Royal South Hants Hospital. Now all the surrounding space was gradually being taken up—unfortunately no more green fields. Large car parks also emerged, surrounded by small trees, which would eventually grow with lots of shrubs and make a pleasant backdrop for patients to see when they looked out of the ward windows.

The Queen came to officially open it. The year was 1974 and it was a televised ceremony. I was one of the lucky ones invited to have afternoon tea with her, I don't know why as I wasn't anyone special. The invite came from Matron and I never did know why I was one of the privileged. Unfortunately though, I could not attend, as I was unwell.

At the time my office was at the Old General Hospital, so I would commute to the East wing. As more offices were installed for the Catering Dept along with another kitchen and more dining rooms, the staff had increased. More catering managers and office staff came along. Eventually John Wane, the catering Manager, gave me a promotion and I joined them in the East Wing as an office manager. I had my own office now.

I enjoyed my post. Ann Cooper was the secretary. Ann Humphries and Betty Bedford worked in the menu office in the afternoon, whilst Wendy Betteridge worked in the mornings with Jill coming along later. Maureen Sharpe worked alongside me but later left, along with Ann the secretary who was to be replaced by Tracy.

Ann Humphries decided much to my delight, to work full-time and did the general office routine. She would take over my position when I retired. I missed Maureen. She was an excellent worker and a good friend. She is now living in France and we keep in touch. At one time we went on a protest march through the streets of Southampton—we were both union minded.

I enjoyed my role in the union as a staff representative and helped to solve many problems. I studied a course at the South-ampton Institute.

Ann settled in really well, she was very reluctant to take the job but I am so glad she did as she proved to be top graded clerical officer and did all that was needed of her. She was another good colleague and friend.

I organised staff parties, which were great fun. We held them in the South Academic dining room and Ann would willingly help to raise money for this yearly event. We would organise raffles, bring and buy, and anything to raise money. Eventually I opened a bank account named 'Staff Party'. A lot of cash was raised and it enabled us to pay for all the food, entertainment, party hats, streamers, balloons and about twenty big raffle prizes.

All of the catering staff were invited and could come with a friend or partner. It was all for free and on top of that they also had the chance of winning a free prize in the raffle. There were lots of prizes, including televisions. About 200 or more people would attend.

Word soon got round the hospital about the Catering party night and hospital staff would pester us to come. Eventually we relented and for a small fee they would be invited but again, the number had to be restricted. This was always a night to remember and it went on for many years.

A committee was formed as we felt it was only fair that the staff could partake in the party arrangements by offering help and suggestions. It became very popular. We needed new ideas and it was great. All of the hard work through the year in our lunch breaks was well worth it when the parties proved to be such a success.

Sadly on my retirement the parties ceased, as nobody wanted the responsibility. After a while the committee disbanded and they were worried about the amount of money that had accumulated in the bank account. They contacted me and suggested we spend it on having a good night out at the theatre. I didn't agree as a lot of old staff had gone, and the new staff would unfairly receive the benefit. I thought it would be more rewarding to give a cheque to the elderly people's unit, and everyone thought this was an excellent idea.

About £800 was donated and this went towards providing new duvets and curtains. The unit was very pleased and the catering staff were very happy.

The bed race was another attraction and a big event in which various Hospitals participated to raise money. For each department, doctors, nurses and staff would enter a bed dressed according to a specific theme they had chosen. The race would start at the South Hants Hospital with a line up of beds. It became a wonderful and amusing sight to see.

With the click of the signal, away they would go, racing through the streets and stopping at various pubs along the way for a glass of beer. Money was collected in tins, which caused a lot of amusement amongst passers by. The race would eventually end at the General Hospital.

It was chaotic when they got back to base, sometimes the fire brigade would be waiting with their hoses accompanied by the catering staff throwing flour bombs, so one can imagine the mess with the water and flour flowing.

At one event the Catering Staff decided to enter and the theme was to be Zulus. Staff were blackened from top to toe with wigs were made out of mops. Chicken bones were stewed and made into necklaces, and skirts made from string were slung around the waist.

The bed looked great, thanks to Bill who made a thatched hut—very impressive. A cauldron hung in the middle of the bed with menus attached. We mustn't forget the pith helmet either. I also made some skeleton heads out of paper-mache that were attached to canes and wired on to the corners of the bed. It really was a good effort.

Another time it was a 'Flintstones' theme. Ryan, aged about eight years old, was pulled in for this and showed his talents in the design and creation of a dinosaur.

Catering staff decided independently to have a cycle run through the forest, which ended at Beaulieu. A lot of money was raised for this event and the cash went to the Ambulance dept who were in need of special equipment. Bill and I seemed to always get involved. We would go on ahead of the cycle run in the car and welcome them at a pub where we would have our lunch.

## CHAPTER ELEVEN

In 1984, at the age of 62 years, my lovely brother Peter died. He committed suicide. The family were devastated. Bill and I rushed to his flat where Marion was recuperating from having her leg amputated. Unfortunately she wasn't in a fit state to deal with the circumstances and so I immediately moved in to look after her and help her cope. Bill did the necessary running around.

Three days later Marion was rushed to hospital and died of a stroke. The days that followed were terrible to bear, the funeral arrangements had to be re-arranged and it ended up with a double funeral. I still think of Pete, I loved him so, and will remember him for all that he did for me and my Mum and Pop in their time of need.

Thank God my dear Mum wasn't alive at this sad time. Don's wife Alice died a month later.

In 1980 we became members of the Tyrrell family history Society, which was founded in 1978. My father's name was Terrell and it is spelt in several different ways such as Turrell, Tirril, Terrell, Tyrrell, Terel etc. There are various meeting places where throughout the year we are able to get together, and one such special day is spent at Rufus Stone in the New Forest. We also have Newsletters sent on a regular basis.

When I first started work at the hospital, the catering manager was a Miss Mallet, later to be followed by Keith Leadbetter and eventually John Wane. There were lots of assistants who eventually moved on and some of these were Lesley Andrews, Anne Kelly, Ken Graham, Marion Germaine, Katie, Sharon, Fiona etc. The girls in the office were great. Betty collated menus in the afternoon and in the early days Ann helped her. Lots of students came and went. My colleagues in the kitchen and dining room were lovely people and I made some great friends and am left with some very happy memories. Alan Saffery—kitchen Superintendent, Lelo—patient meals supervisor, Joan Adams—dining room supervisor; they all contributed to my happy days at work.

A party was organised on my 60th birthday, with a wonderful farewell when I actually retired. It was a big secret.

The day arrived and my office was decorated throughout. A pair of specs, about fourteen inches in length and bright red, had been made. They actually had half lenses and glass was inserted, a replica of the ones I wore in the office that were always perched on my nose. It obviously caused a great laugh.

Only essential work was done that day, the staff had been working hard for days to keep things up to scratch. Lots of good luck messages adorned the desks. I was in an excited dream world.

Lunch break came and I was whisked to the Truffles Restaurant. It was next to the staff dining room and staff would use it on special occasions—this was one such occasion.

When I entered I had the shock of my life, sat at the Head table was John Ramshaw, the District Catering Manager, and alongside him, my Bill and then Lesley. Two long tables ran parallel and there sat ex-colleagues, catering managers and assistants, clerical staff and secretaries etc. Also present were all my work colleagues responsible for this wonderful day.

Ann Humphries and Tracy the secretary were the ones that instigated this surprise. It must have been quite an experience to undertake. So many people came from far and wide—London, Wales, Yorkshire, I just cannot remember all, Ann and Tracy were such good friends of mine both at work, and personally and they have continued to keep in touch. We often meet up at each other's houses.

The surprises continued—Sally Marchant, the pastry Chef, had made a beautiful cake. Sally is now married and lives in Scotland with her own teashop and specialist wedding cake business.

The meal was superb and wine flowed. Alan Saffery, the kitchen superintendent, was responsible for this side of the event, along with Joan Adams, the dining room supervisor, Beryl Andrews—Truffles supervisor, and the Ganymede supervisor—Rosie Laxton. Lelo Bathard had already retired.

It was quite late when we returned to the office, everybody disbanded and I was left feeling a little forlorn. I packed all of my belongings and presents.

One or two of the staff came in and waylaid me, wanting to chat. I was filled with so many emotions that I wanted to leave, but someone made a cup tea and more talk flowed. Then, I was asked to pop into the kitchen as someone could not get away from their post and wanted to say goodbye.

When I arrived I was whisked away once again into another room, and lo and behold there was the kitchen, dining room and Ganymede staff, along with Ryan and Elliott. I was greeted with presents, and there were one or two speeches accompanied by more food and drinks (the catering staff had finished their shifts by then). Flowers were presented too, and then the big surprise.

John Ramshaw presented me with some Wrought iron white garden furniture, from all the staff in the department. I was overwhelmed.

Eventually I managed to return to my office with Lesley and Bill. I looked around—this was it. Silently, I said goodbye with a flood of memories engulfing me. I reluctantly closed the door, and was finally on my way

Then another shock awaited me, a long red carpet had been laid and colleagues were there in abundance. I turned my head and lo and behold, my carriage awaited me, standing proudly with notices on the front and back saying "FAREWELL". The horse was raring to go with the driver, adorned with a top hat and whip, alongside. It was only me holding back.

Eventually we trotted off home but I made sure Elliott sat by my side. Goodbye General Hospital you have left me lots of memories.

The next day Ann and Tracy visited us and we had lunch in the garden using my newly acquired garden furniture. It was sweet of them to come—it helped me so much. It took me several days to get over all the excitement and settle down but fortunately Bill had already retired and so was able to take me out and about.

I enrolled in a ceramic class at Romsey where I met some lovely people and enjoyed creating on the pottery wheel. Hazel taught us, and I really looked forward to my Thursday afternoons. She was also brilliant at flower arranging, and had set up a studio in the gardens of her house. Here we had Saturday workshops.

After this I had a go at learning sugar craft at evening classes and progressed well with the skill, so joined the Sugar craft Guild. I made and decorated lots of birthday and anniversary cakes and was quite pleased with myself when I made a three-tiered wedding cake.

Over the years we had become good friends with Lena and Bill. We would often stay with them and their three lovely children—Irene, Alan, and Teresa—at their beautiful house in Marchwood. We were very fond of them all and store some wonderful memories.

We attended all of the children's weddings and got to know their relations very well over the years. Teresa married a man named Trevor and they are very dear in my heart.

My Bill had a wonderful bond with Teresa. They shared the same birthday, and often enjoyed arguing in a friendly way over politics. Teresa and Trevor live in a wonderful house in Hythe Marina. Lauren their daughter has just celebrated her 21st birthday.

## CHAPTER TWELVE

We often enjoyed many holidays with Lena and Bill. Lots of these were taken before we retired. Our very first holiday abroad was thirty-five years ago. It was in Majorca when Lesley was about sixteen years old and her friend Ann came along. They were both apprentice hairdressers.

As the years went by, many more vacations followed with Lena and Bill—Malta, Austria, France, Yugoslavia, Germany, and Romania. We also visited France many times from the North to the South. It all started when Lena had a French student stay with her in the summer. It was the time Lesley was married, the year 1974.

I could not settle after Lesley wed and as we had time off from work, Lena invited us to her house. The French student, Brigitte, was there and we got acquainted. We took her out and about visiting various areas of interest and beauty spots. This friendship continued over the years and she would often come back to Lena and Bill's along with her parents and other relations.

We were all invited to Cherbourg to stay with Brigitte's uncle and aunt, Michelle and Brigitte. Lena, Bill, my Bill and I had a lovely holiday with them. They were both teachers and spoke very good English.

Another year we travelled to the south of France and the coastal resort of Sab-de-a-lon, where we met another aunt and uncle, Robert and Annie. The hospitality was wonderful. A party was arranged when we arrived and we sang and danced the night away—it was the first time we had met. We stayed the night, and in the morning motored further into Mouranx, a little town nestled below the Pyrenees Mountains.

Paulette and Gaston were Brigitte's Mum and dad and were absolutely delightful people. We spent about ten days with them and what a wonderful holiday is was. They took us all over the place, even into the Pyrenees where the mountains were laden with snow. Up and up we motored in their doormanville, it was breathtaking looking down on the beautiful lakes, it looked so unreal.

Eventually we reached Pandora—the separation point between Spain and France. On we went, and eventually got to our picnic area where the wine came out and Gaston sunk some bottles in the snow. The sun was shining and it was very hot as we were lying there in the snow, eating,
drinking and enjoying ourselves.

Another time we motored into Spain and found that it was not as commercialised as we had thought, in fact it was very traditionally Spanish. We stayed the night and obviously were something of an oddity as we received many stares from the local people.

All the shops were shut throughout lunch and the afternoon. We were sitting in the Square and the children were heading home from school, many were skipping and we joined in. The men were strolling to and fro and the women, mostly dressed in black clothes, were busy gossiping. It was just a typical day, no rushing around, but we loved the atmosphere.

When our holiday ended at Mourenx we said goodbye to our lovely friends and motored back, again staying en-route in Sab-de-alon with Annie and Robert and with Brigitte and Michelle at Beaumont Cherbourg before finally getting the ferry home to Portsmouth.

Another time Bill and I popped over to Cherbourg to see our French friends. Bill and Lena could not come this particular time. Brigitte now had a little girl called Sylvie, who was about 4years old. She absolutely adored Bill and followed him wherever he went.

As Brigitte and Gaston were teaching in the village school they asked if we would like to visit the classrooms, this we did and it was quite an experience. Brigitte introduced us to the children aged about eleven to twelve years. We could not speak French and the pupils were at that time being taught English, she asked them to ask us questions, which they duly fired at us.

One lad asked our ages, the teacher interrupted, and said they must not ask that question. Bill said that it was alright and perfectly fair because he had previously asked some of the children their ages. He told them he was fifty-nine years old and within a few days he would be sixty. He was very impressed with another lad who was asked what sport he liked playing, and replied: 'cricket'. It particularly impressed Bill, as it was a sport that they don't play in France. Obviously the lad knew it was a sport played in the U.K and said what he thought Bill would like to hear. His name was Simon Verrier and I still keep in touch. He visited us a few years ago and brought Ann his wife along to meet us. Simon is a teacher and has two lovely little girls, Garance aged five, and Ester—aged about ten months.

Young Brigitte, who started this friendship when she was a student in England, is a Paediatrician with a family of three boys.

After we returned home to England it was nearing the day of Bills birthday. He received a card from two of the French pupils we had met, it impressed and touched him very much and he sent them a post-card to thank them. A few days later a deluge of cards came through the letterbox about forty odd, from two classes of pupils. It was wonderful, but we then had a problem on our hands because Bill insisted that we write to all of them separately as he had done with the previous two.

So a postcard campaign started and we searched the shops and visited various towns to obtain different views etc. We managed to get what we needed and then it was getting down to replying. What a task, but we succeeded.

From then on correspondence started. Obviously some of the pupils opted out after a while but others continued, and one or two came to stay with us. I still write to them now but now they are grown and married with children.

It has brought great pleasure through the years, just last week I had a postcard from Geraldine Lourent who was on holiday with her family. This was one of the girls who stayed with us all those years ago.

About thirty-five years ago Lena and Bill had a nineteen-year-old Japanese student named Kioshi to stay. He stayed for about six months and often visited us. Kioshi was very sweet on Lesley and took her out for an evening meal.

Lesley was shy and not interested but he became a good friend to all of us. He eventually returned home and we corresponded. Lena and Bill went to London and met his sister who was a famous pop star in Japan and a beautiful girl.

Years later Kioshi came to visit, this time as a mature man of about fifty years. He was staying at a hotel in London and was on a business meeting with several of his colleagues from Japan. He would be then on his way to Paris the next day.

It was indeed lovely to see him and talk about old times he took many pictures. Kioshi was devastated to see Bill paralysed and unable to speak but he warmed to him very much and chatted which was nice. Bill was so happy to see him.

He came on another visit with his beautiful wife Junco and stayed with Teresa and Trevor. Lesley and Graham came to the house with Ryan, Elliott and Yo. It was a lovely afternoon with them all. We keep in touch via E-Mail.

Malta was a lovely place with many old historical buildings and churches to visit. The people are English speaking and very friendly and the beaches and hotels were great. We went with Lena and Bill, and managed to meet up with an old colleague, Maria, who had worked with us both at the General Hospital.

Maria had a lovely sense of humour, and had originally come from Malta. She married an Englishman and settled in England where they had a son. However, after he had grown up and left school, her marriage broke up and eventually she decided to return to her homeland to be with her family.

So whilst we were holidaying in Malta we contacted her and asked if she would visit us at our hotel, which she did. Maria wanted us to visit her home at Valencia and meet her family and we agreed to do so on another day. The day eventually arrived and Maria and her sister met us. Before we could go into her home we had to cover our heads and visit the local church to say a prayer.

She mentioned that some of the locals would be present in the church, and would turn and gaze at us, but that we were to take no notice. They would just be inquisitive and knew that we were coming. The villagers were not used to foreigners where they lived and probably some would never leave their local village. We were made to feel very important.

After church we walked to the house. It was a very narrow white building perched on a sloping hill with the door opening out onto the roadway.

We came to just a door, there were no windows, and entered this quaint little abode into a tiny little entrance room with a wicker chair and stairs in front. We climbed a few and came to a bedroom. Another few stairs and another bedroom, a few more stairs and there was a sitting room another few stairs and there was the kitchen, one walked through the kitchen and came out to a beautiful patio area where we could see over Malta.

A lovely sight met our eyes. White buildings surrounded us. This is where the Maltese sat, as we would in our own gardens. We were all intrigued, and loved both the place, and the people.

We were told of a lot of history about the war when our soldiers (my brother Len was one of them) helped to defend the Island. The navy had ships berthed there and a statue is erected of a sailor and child. The whole Island was very upset when they eventually pulled out.

Len, my dear brother, survived the war, but has since died. When Len was stationed in Malta, my dear dad was very ill and was going to die. The Army tried their utmost to fly Len home to say goodbye to his dad, but unfortunately at that stage of the war they could not get the planes out.

Len had not seen his dad for about five years. He was already away in the Middle East before the war started, as he was a regular soldier. When war broke out, Len continued to fight in various countries.

Our German holiday had its highlights, we were on a coach tour right through to the Rhine and on the way we stopped and stayed the night in Brussels.

Cologne was very interesting and the cathedral, awesome. We coached on down to the Rhine where our Hotel was right on the edge of the river. It was lovely at night when the boats would chug-chug along, passing many castles that looking so enchanting with their lights twinkling away in the twilight. We did a lot of tours that were very interesting but also very tiring.

Another time we flew to Romania and had a two-part holiday, one of which was sat a skiing resort. We stayed in a beautiful hotel in the mountains. The slopes were empty of skiers as it was summertime, but we were able to go up and down on the cable cars and see the sights. Romania at that time was a poor country. Most of the food, such as meat and fruit, was imported and prioritised mainly for the tourists. The Romanians were on a very poor diet and we didn't enjoy the food that much. A lot of it was cooked maize that was mashed and stuffed with ivy leaves. Bread had a sour taste.

The black market was rife and there were different shopping areas where the locals could not shop, such as the dollar shops. If they were caught buying from the wrong shops, it was immediate imprisonment.

The next part of the holiday was spent in a lovely hotel by the sea. There were several of them in a complex with a purpose made beach. The Romanians were not allowed in, it was very strange. In the rural areas, the grass was cut with scythes and very small hayricks were stacked.

There little technology and everywhere seemed years behind, for example, the carpets were pulled from the hotels and the staff would beat them. The roadways everywhere were spotlessly clean and swept with brooms daily. We were told that they kept themselves years behind as it enabled every-one to have a job. I didn't quite believe that.

The waiters in the hotel would slide up to us to see if we could get them cigarettes. It was so much cheaper in the shops we visited—we managed to help, but it was a chance we took because at night soldiers would man the beaches, and private detectives were about. We all had to be on the alert.

One day when we were walking in the shopping area, Bill was approached and asked to sell his camera. We swiftly walked on, didn't want to get involved. It was pointless going into the shops to buy gifts to bring home as they were very austere and it was very dark inside—no bright lights at all and only few things to buy.

I cannot remember the year we were there—at a guess I would say it was the seventies—so maybe it has changed now, I cannot say. Everything was done to make visitors comfortable as the tourist industry was needed to bring revenue to this poor country. Most of the inhabitants were very glum, obviously they had nothing to be happy about -it was so sad.

It was so different when we went to Austria. We travelled by coach and did not stay in a hotel with the rest of the party, opting instead to stay with the Austrians. We were so glad we made this decision; it was wonderful, so exhilarating.

The village was perched very high in the alpine area; we seemed to travel round and round and up and up, what a journey. It was dark when we arrived, so we did not see the beauty that was to greet us. The next morning tucked high in the Alps was our village of Leonhard. The house to which we were allocated was perched at the top of the village, and surrounded by forest. It looked down on the rest of the houses, adorned with window boxes full of flowers (mainly geraniums), and the roads were cobbled. Nestled at the bottom of the village was a dear little church with a cemetery attached, we noticed that all the gravestones were black. A little old lady would be there every day attending a grave or graves.

The family surname was Shautsberger, and the lady of the house was called Giselle. Her daughter had the same name and was a teacher who could speak English, which was a bonus as she met us and introduced us to her mother. She then left and went away to where ever she lived, it wasn't in the village.

It was fun communicating from then on but we managed. In the house we had rooms upstairs for sleeping and separating these two rooms was a large landing adapted to a small kitchen, so we were completely separated.

Our beds were a dream, the linen stunningly white the pillows large and square completed with a snowy white duvet. It was years ago when we visited Austria and our bed linen at home was totally different, duvets were not around. Our beds at home were made up of sheets and blankets and on top was an eiderdown.

Giselle's beds really impressed me, and I soon followed suit with all the linen snowy white. Years ago all sheets were white, but just after the war it changed and colour sheets came in. Our main meals were eaten at the hotel including all socialising and parties.

We ate our breakfast at the house. Giselle would pop to the local bakers, which was situated just below us. We could smell the lovely aroma of bread and cakes; she would also purchase succulent rolls and cold meats for our breakfast meal.

On the first Sunday of our stay, we were introduced to Giselle's husband. His name eludes me. He was a small, slight man and was dressed in the traditional Tyrolean costume, the usual procedure when going to church. He had his two blond grandsons with him, about six years and eight years old. He did not stay long and clicked his heels when he left. We were all so amused.

Many walks in the forest were enjoyed and other days we visited various towns, villages and Ski-Slopes. We saw some wonderful sights.

One of the trips was to Vienna. As the Cathedral was in the process of renovation we could not visit—there was a lot of structure surrounding it. In the middle of the town was a bandstand and the musicians were playing Straus music such as the Viennese Waltz. White wigs were worn and the musicians also dressed in the appropriate costumes. We stood there a long time and listened, it was magical.

Our intentions were to go back to Austria one day and stay with Giselle, but unfortunately it never happened. We have kept in touch and exchanged Christmas cards and small gifts. She would always write a few words in German and her daughter would add a few lines in English.

Our last holiday spent abroad with Bill and Lena was Yugoslavia, now named Croatia. This again was a lovely place to spend a holiday, beautiful clear sea and lovely hotels. The place where we stayed was Cilipi, not too far from Dubrovnik, a lovely old medieval town. One could look down on the sea that nearly encircled the town.

In later years there was terrible devastation when the country split and a civil war erupted after their leader Tito died. Yugoslavia became Croatia and Serbia, how could such lovely people fight against each other.

The British army sent troops out to help. The war was nasty, buildings were destroyed, and many people died.

Help was needed and lorries of food and clothes were sent from Britain. I tried to help in a small way. I collected shoeboxes from shops in town and asked friends, relatives and anyone that came my way if they could donate food, toys, cosmetics, paper, pencils and clothes etc.

I thought I would send out a couple of boxes, but it went further than that. I was inundated! I began packing—everything went out in the conservatory and I wrapped all the boxes with the white side of some wallpaper, labelling and decorating each individually, Boy, Girl, Man, Woman, or baby. I divided the children's parcels into age groups. A lorry was sent to the house and my first consignment was four hundred parcels.

Not long after, another appeal went out from the Advertiser local paper so I managed to do about another 300 boxes. It was sent out to Yugoslavia in time for Xmas, It was hard work as I was looking after Bill who was confined to the house, but I had achieved what I needed to do.

In one of the parcels I put a little note explaining where the goodies came from. One day I received a letter from a schoolgirl who had received a parcel. She had to be evacuated from Dubrovnik and I think she lost the family home so she went to live with her grandmother who lived in Cilipi, where we had previously had our lovely holiday. What a coincidence.

I still write to Marina, who is now married with a baby. Over the years she sent photographs of her family and spoke of her school days, college days and work. She also sent pictures of the celebrations when they were able to return to Dubrovnik. This was very rewarding.

## CHAPTER THIRTEEN

Time to move on with retirement, and Bill had thrown himself into many projects—keeping garden up to scratch, building a conservatory, and teaching himself to paint with watercolours at which he became very proficient.

His main delight was being with our grandsons, Ryan and Elliott. He liked to fetch them from Mountbatten School and take them into the forest.

They loved to see the wildlife and would sit patiently waiting for deer to appear, but the highlight was the fried egg sandwiches that Grandpa had lovingly made, and they would soon be hungrily devoured. Bill had made sure they had lovely chunky bread just baked at the bakery, a fried egg placed inside and the sandwich wrapped in tin foil to keep warm.

He helped them with their studies, and they enjoyed building various projects with him. At one time they both had ferrets (pole-cats) and were intrigued with the long outside run he built enabling them to chase each other and have fun. They even had a two-storey house to sleep in.

Ryan and Elliott loved their ferrets named 'Cheever' and 'Tito' and would spend a lot of their spare moments with them. Unfortunately one day someone stole them. They appealed in the local echo for their return, but no luck. Bill could not rest and spent days trying to find them.

Bill continued his watercolour painting and I did courses on cake making and sugar craft, de-coupage plus many more crafts. I enjoyed sugar craft and belonged to the local sugar-craft guild where I became the treasurer.

Our Family—Bill—Me—Ryan—Lesley—Elliott and Graham 1982

We would meet once a month and have lectures and workshops learning the art of making sugar flowers so delicate and so real—it was a wonderful form of art. I did not think I would ever reach the standard expected but I did, and eventually was able to make beautiful sprays of flowers. They looked wonderful on wedding cakes, sometimes imitating the bridal bouquet.

The actual cake making courses incorporated icing the cakes either with royal icing or roll out icing. I continued to make birthday and wedding cakes and I also made lots of friends.

Sadly on October 2nd 1991, at the age of 72, Bill had a massive stroke. We were all so devastated. There was not much hope over the first 24 hours, and we prepared ourselves for the worse.

Lesley and I stayed with him. He was paralysed completely down his right side, could not swallow or speak or recognise us. I stayed with him as long as I could. We would visit early in the morning and stay as late as possible in the evening.

The first few days I would damp his lips with a sponge that gradually increased to eating a little jelly, then soft foods etc until he could eat normally. Eventually recognition came and I would talk and talk to him hoping he would respond but the communication was not there.

A Speech Therapist came on the scene and therapy began. He also had lots of physio and one day the physiotherapist encouraged Bill to try a few steps with a walking stick to balance him. I could not watch this procedure—it was a very long process.

Motivation came to the fore in my mind, and as soon as Bill was able to sit up in a chair I was encouraging him to use his left hand and write. This seemed an impossible task, as at times he could not comprehend what I meant. I would go to lunch and tell him I expected something to be done on my return.

I knew that Bill could not do this alone but I was always hoping. I would write his name down, but again it did not mean anything. I persevered, and every day would write his name and ask him to copy it.

At last I was greeted with at least something, he had written the odd formed letter but the rest was scribble. It was very rewarding though. We did not get very far, but pressed on. There were no miracles, but improvements were beginning to show although very slowly.

Copying his name came first and although it was barely legible it was a breakthrough. Other words then followed with odd letters missing, some back to front, etc.

Life in the hospital became part of my life. Often Lesley would pop in early in the morning and we would bath Bill. The nurses showed us how to hoist him into the bath and after a little practice we became quite proficient. It was laughable in the beginning though—my darling was often left straddled in the air as we giggled through our panic. Bill would go along with it—I think he understood we were trying our very best.

Lesley and I would come out of the bathroom dishevelled with hot red faces and Bill would be sat in his wheelchair, smartly dressed and all preened up, ready for the battles of the day. There was many a smile from the nurses.

We would then strip his bed and make it up with lovely white fresh sheets. Lesley would retreat back to her home to look after her family and prepare to go to work in the evening and I would stay to help in any way I could to motivate Bill. Graham helped all he could on the home front, with the boys still at school aged about 14 and 15 years.

One day, Doctor Sterling, the consultant, said that Bill would have to move on from the Medical ward to the Geriatric Department, I was absolutely gutted. In my small way of thinking I realised he could not have the stimulation amongst the elderly, even though he was then seventy-two himself.

In the medical ward he was amongst various age groups, and the patients would often chat to him and he would listen and smile. They would also look out for him when I wasn't around and would call the nurse if help was needed. It was sad that Bill could not comprehend how to use his bell.

Bill also suffered from a hiatus hernia. Before the stroke, he was able to cope with this, but now if bile erupted from it he could easily choke and it worried me. I was terribly concerned and took my concerns to his doctor who soon put me at ease and made sure his medication was regularly given. He also decided to turn his bed back to front, which would draw attention to his problem to any new staff around.

The patients were often his voice and so when he was left I felt at ease. Fortunately the choking never occurred—it would have been devastating if it had, as Bill would panic knowing that he could not help himself.

And so I appealed to doctor Sterling to keep him on his ward or to be transferred to the Rehabilitation unit, but unfortunately they could not accept him as the ward was for patients under the age of sixty-five years. Southampton General Hospital did not have a stroke ward at that time but I am so pleased to say they have now

Bill had been admitted to the medical ward because he was already under the care of a specialist, Doctor Sterling, with his lung condition. I pleaded and pleaded and eventually won doctor Sterling over. He broke the rules to let Bill stay and recuperation began.

He did remark that I was actually nursing Bill and taking the strain off the nurses, so his bed was kept in the corner of the ward. Lesley and I were so happy and we appreciated it so much.

Over the years I persevered and did not give up. I realised it was hard work for Bill and it was rewarding that he would always try. Not a lot of improvement came however, and so obviously he had reached as far as he could go.

He was able to sign birthday cards on his own and could write 'with love' if he copied. It would not come from Bill voluntarily and at times he was confused. He also had the other obstacle of having to use his left hand. Figures were a different matter. He could write them down on his own if I called the numbers and he could even add up, so strange. The Speech Therapist said it was most unusual but she had heard of it.

At an appointment with her for an assessment, she told Bill that he would never be able to speak again as the stroke had hit the brain at a point where there was no recovery. We did not give up though and he would manage to repeat any word I asked him to say. Sometimes it was understandable and sometimes not, but it did not matter—I understood and communication was fine for us.

So the days slipped by and Bill was gradually improving, the physiotherapist had him walking he was trying so hard to take a step. In between therapies I took Bill out in his wheelchair around the hospital. Up and down the corridors we went and I would sing along and often he would join in. This was so extraordinary from someone who could not speak and when it first happened I rushed back to tell everyone. The Speech Therapist said that this could happen. I must add that Bill wasn't a singer and it was very out of character that on these occasions he would join in with me when I sang. I would sing a verse and he would maybe finish it or just a few words. They were wonderful moments for me.

I adapted this as a way of bringing a little fun into Bill's life. It was so rewarding when he joined in or finished off a line when I stopped. It was so wonderful for me to actually hear his voice. It had to be at the right time and songs that he knew and he would only sing along with me—he could not sing on his own and he couldn't do it with an audience.

It continued for the rest of his life and to this day I still sing these songs around the house hoping I would hear that dear voice. It might only have been a couple of words but it was music to my ears.

The nurses were wonderful to Bill and they all became his friends, even the tea-lady knew how many sugars he needed in his tea. Life was as pleasant as it could be under the circumstances.

Patients would come and go and we made many acquaintances. I would help them as much as I could and would often fetch and carry for them. I would leave Bill at about 9pm and trot on down to casualty to wait for Lesley who was working at reception. We would eventually return home together—at that time I was sleeping at Lesley's house.

Unfortunately we had a break in at my house, a video recorder was stolen and Bill's sheepskin coat. The double-glazed glazing in the window at the back of the lounge had to be replaced. Lesley had the added burden of sorting this and as it all happened in the first week of Bill's stroke, it was a lot to take.

## CHAPTER FOURTEEN

There were a lot of ups and downs in the hospital with Bill's health, but he courageously fought each crisis A happy day came—I was able to give Bill some good news about me.

In 1981 I was diagnosed with cancer of the uterus. I had radium cesiums implanted and had to lay still and flat on my back for a week in a bed at the radiotherapy unit. It wasn't a very pleasant time. Little food passed my lips, and visitors were not allowed in my room, as I was radioactive. An iron grid blocked the doorway where they could stand and talk.

After a week, the time came for the radium to be taken away from my body. I remember it very well—it was a few minutes past two in the early hours of the morning. After the job was finished the implant, whatever it was, it was quickly immersed in an iron receptacle and whisked away by a porter.

The next day I was allowed a most wanted bath and then allowed home where I was to rest for six weeks. An operation was then performed and I had a total hysterectomy at the Princess Ann Hospital.

I recuperated at Barton-on-Sea and I remember being very unwell. Eventually I went to my sister in Dorset, but had to come home, as I wasn't well enough to stay.

Eventually as time went on checks were made every three months at the two hospitals, then reduced to six months and eventually a year. Ten years on and this was my last visit at the Radiotherapy Unit—I was given the all clear.

The doctor shook my hand and congratulated me, I was cured and he did not want to see me again. Bill was thrilled with this news. Not all has been well since, as it left me with problems with the bowel and bladder but I am cured of cancer and can put up with the rest.

Bill was so happy with the news and we hugged.

After about five months Bill was allowed to come home to be looked after by me. The Occupational Therapist and the physiotherapist came to our home to see what would be required to meet his needs. One little hiccup was that he obviously could not get up the stairs and so a suggestion was made that the bed was brought downstairs.

This was not going to be the near normal life that I wanted for Bill. I was asked if I could purchase a stair lift. At this stage I had never seen one but now they are widely advertised on the television and if Social Services have them installed where they are required.

Over the years of caring I learnt a lot. Although resources were available to meet Bill's needs and requirements, they unfortunately had to be fought for and one only found this out along the way. I passed a lot of this information on to other people; yes it was available but one had to go through various routes to get there and at times it wasn't easy.

For instance, had I have known of these difficulties I would have made sure that Bill was able to have a stair lift through Social Services. I would have stuck to my guns and no way would I have let him come home until it was installed. Instead I had to purchase a second-hand one, as this was all I could afford.

The British Legion helped a little with the finances. It wasn't only the purchasing of the stair-lift, it was the actual upkeep and servicing involved each year, which was fifty pounds. Also, when it got stuck or went wrong in other ways we would have to pay another fifty pounds for an out-of-hours call out and cover the cost of any additional work involved.

Over the years there was a lot of cost down to us and we had to pay the top rate for his care because my darling received a war-pension. He was penalised so many times. I could not believe it. I was informed when Bill had his stroke that his pension was not to be disclosed for financial purposes. He wasn't taxed on it as it was compensation and not categorized as income.

The fight was on; I explored all avenues and even exploited the local media. I learned that all over the country it was down to local councils whether they took this money into consideration or not, some did and some didn't.

I didn't give up. I approached Southampton Council once again and managed to get two thirds disregarded, with the promise that they would eventually disregard the lot (it has yet to happen). I did win part of my battle and it also helped other war disabled veterans in Southampton. Obviously they would be quite elderly and there weren't many left.

Now with various wars cropping up there will be many young disabled military personnel and in years to come they will probably need the extra help in their old age. If I can help in my small way to stop the councils taking their pensions to help pay for health cost, I will.

I still cannot understand why there wasn't any legislation on this matter. Why should councils such as Southampton decide when they budgeted to discriminate these war-pensioners against others in the country?

When my husband was a prisoner of war for five long years, returning very disabled, we struggled for years on this pension. What happened to the five years of wages he never had in the camps? They were issued with camp money that was useless when out of the camp. His youth had come and gone, like a whisper in the wind. He did not complain. I have now taken on the roll of complainer 60 years on. I must emphasise that 'Prisoners of War' are treated so differently in other countries.

Throughout our life, we did not bare any malice against the German War Machine, especially Bill. I feel very angry that his own country did not come forward in the twilight of his years when he needed help.

This is where my fight began; I then had to leave it for a couple of years as Bill became so ill, but now it is to continue. I shall notify my M.P. and see where it will go from there. We took out insurance with the government in 1947 for our health needs and paid all our working life, we have been lead up the garden path.

The big day was here and I was so excited. Charlie, my brother-in-law, had previously decorated the bedroom. The carpets had been ripped up, new ones laid and beds were replaced. We had slept in a double bed but this had to be replaced by two singles owing to Bill's disabilities. The room fortunately was bright and very inviting.

I arranged a party on the ward, well actually it was in the Sister's office, and goodies were purchased from the catering dept along with bits and pieces collected along the way. A lovely cake was made and decorated with thanks to all the staff on D5. Bill had been there for many months and we had both made many friends there. In a way it was a joyful and sad time, we were so grateful for all the work that had helped Bill to progress.

The Occupational Therapist, Speech Therapist, Domestics and many others came in and out, had some nibbles and said their goodbyes. I was able to say my thanks personally to all of the lovely staff that had helped my Bill in his struggles.

The great day had arrived my Bill was coming home. A nurse came home with us to settle him in. It was arranged that twilight nurses would come in the evenings to help and see Bill safely into bed. He had to be propped up in bed and so had to have many pillows. The district nurse came in twice a week to give Bill a bath. A bath seat was installed over the bath enabling him to be washed and then showered. With the help of the nurse he would be swung round and helped out. Bill was able to sit at the sink and clean his teeth and also dry shave using his left hand. Gradually he became quite proficient at this.

Another journey had begun. Social services stepped in and wanted me to have more help but I did not want the intrusion.

How ignorant I was not to accept—but this was all so new to me. I wanted to look after Bill and help him in every way possible. This I did lovingly for three years and then my health began to deteriorate which involved several operations. So to be able to keep Bill with me I needed the extra help.

A carer, Nickie, came in every day early in the morning to help Bill out of bed and bath him on his bath seat. Twilight nurses continued to help him to bed at night. District Nursing had moved out. Care in the Community was beginning to change.

My days were spent helping and motivating Bill as much as possible. We would sit in our workshop and he would try with his artwork. At times my darling would get terribly frustrated, first of all he had to practice with a paintbrush in his left hand and the paralysed right hand would lay dormant. Colours did not mean much, and his work would end up a mess.

I would sit by and carry on with my hobbies whilst gently encouraging Bill. Fortunately he did not give up and one day a picture immerged, we were both over the moon.

It was hard work for him, the concentration was immense and it would leave him very tired. This had taken a long time but he had achieved it. At last he had something he could immerse himself into which could only be good. When he was tired he would push it away.

I accepted this and did not push him any further, but we were together and life was good as it could be.

Bill would gaze into the garden and enjoy the wildlife. He would also be interested in the hobbies I was partaking in, especially when I was building a dolls house. If I got stuck on something I would ask his advice. Obviously Bill could not answer, so I would steer it along the lines of saying, "If I did this would that be right?" and so on and so on, and I would know by the expressions on his face if it was O.K. Many times a great big grin would emerge and he would look at me, and that look would say, "Whatever are you trying to do?" He would laugh and I would laugh too—it was fun.

If only Bill could write down what he would have loved to say, it would have been so easy. Unfortunately it was never to be but I managed the art of communicating with him quite well. The dolls house still needs to be completed and is on my 'one of the little things to do' list. I loved watching him persevering with his art and one day I sat with him and painted a picture—the first ever. Bill guided me. It was Colehill in Shaftsbury and I had it framed and it is with Bill's collection on the wall. This is something else I want to do—paint watercolours.

Lesley was able to take me food shopping and we were able to leave Bill for an hour. He was able to go to the toilet on his own, so all was well. On arriving home we would take him out in the car for lunch and often a spin round in the country.

I also tried some driving lessons and did very well. If I was gone longer than an hour Bill would be in quite an agitated mood when I returned, so I would try not to let that happen. I managed to get to test standard, but then completely lost my nerve. I became very anxious when driving, and so spoke to my G.P. about it and he advised me to give it a rest for a while.

I took his advice but I did not return to driving. It would have been a great asset, but it was never to be—my nerve had gone.

Sandra Lawton came on the scene. She ran the local stroke group and visited us, mentioning all of the good it could do for Bill if he attended. On approaching him unfortunately, he flatly refused. Sandra did not give up though, she asked if she could bring along a young man to have a cup of tea and a chat. I agreed and this is where Kevin came into our lives. He was in his early thirties and had suffered a terrible accident a few years back, causing head injuries. He was hospitalised for a very long time.

His disabilities were much the same as stroke. He spoke with a little lisp and could only walk with a walking stick. Kevin was blessed with a wonderful sense of humour and this type of humour certainly made Bill laugh.

He visited on his own for a few weeks as a friend and always demanded his cup of tea as he entered the house. He would play dominoes with Bill, which was a very slow process. Kevin would laugh and say that Bill must have cheated to be able to win the game, as he was so good.

To get a cup of tea Kevin would mischievously say that Bill had wanted it. He was a loveable rogue and there was always laughter around when he came.

Gradually he persuaded Bill to join the stroke club and promised to come and get him on the early visits. He attended for a while but decided it wasn't for him. It was sad really as, again, he had made many friends and I know he did not dislike it there, but I understood his frustration. His lack of speech and communication skills amongst people in a crowd was much too much for him. Apparently if there was a lot of chat around Bill would get confused. I think it sounded like one big buzz. We discovered this when the family came to visit. He would put his hand up if we were all chatting and then indicate for one person to speak at a time. One to one was fine.

We did go on a trip to Hayling-Island with the Stroke Association. People came from different parts of the country. We were housed in chalets and took over a holiday camp. It was good for Bill and me to be able to get away, but I needed help and I paid for two Twilight nurses, Chris and Lyn, to help us out. Of course Sandra was there with her group and also Mac, her husband. We were there for a few days and it was a break for me not having to cook, etc. With Bill being in the sole care of the carers, it was great for both of us.

I met a couple that came from Lymington, and I was intrigued to see the lady whizzing around in an Electric wheel chair. I had seen odd ones about but they were more of a clumsy nature. Anyhow we got chatting and I became interested in the chair. The man was pleased to pass on the information I needed to know.

Bill had a trial run, it was great to see him darting all over the place and being completely independent. He managed the controls very well and I decided there and then, that this was to be for Bill. We were told it was easily transferable in and out of the car as the batteries (of which there were two) could be taken out separately and the chair could then be folded and placed in a car. It was heavy but it could be managed.

On returning home we began the process of purchasing one. The homework had been done, so I didn't have that hassle and soon Bill had his electric wheelchair. It was a lovely birthday gift and life was to become a lot better for him.

He was at last independent when we went out for the day, he actually hated being pushed about. Lesley and I could now take him to large stores to do our shopping and he would dart everywhere on his own, it was great for us all. Electric chairs and scooters of all types are now in abundance.

The next stage was to see if the Council could put down some dropped curbs around our area, this would enable Bill to go around the estate on his own. After a lot of difficult negotiations, the curbs were installed.

Bill had to be persuaded to go out on his own. He knew, as we all did, that neighbours would stop and chat and as he couldn't partake in conversation it was a big hurdle to get over. A little gentle persuasion was needed and so I walked out with him in the beginning as I had been along this road so many times.

Obviously people would stop and chat, but with me accompanying him it wasn't so bad. Gradually I was able to step back and the day soon came when he was away on his own. He would not be gone for long and eventually would ride through into the back garden and sit in the sunshine. In the early days I would keep looking out for him. I was so nervous. The day soon arrived when I could relax and let go.

Wednesday was the day when Lesley was off work and she would take us both out. It became our special day. She was the rock I leaned on. Without her, we would have been confined to the house.

We visited many places—the shops, the forest, and the beach where we would stroll along the prom and all enjoy lunch. Bill would cope very well. We all had our favourite places and The New Forest was one. One day on the journey we popped into a supermarket and purchased three hot chickens cooked on the spit. When we arrived at the forest, operation devouring commenced. Out came the napkins and we tucked in, tearing our lunch to pieces. Bill absolutely loved every moment—we were all greasy but who cared, we were tucked away with bushes surrounding us. Soon the horses, cows, and birds that were flying about hoping to get a morsel or two interrupted us. It was a really fun day, one I shall always keep in my book of memories.

Nina, one of the twilight nurses, brought this to the fore when she was helping Bill to bed one evening and often laughed with Bill over it. He would remember and laugh with her.

Our friend Beryl would visit every other Monday. Bill would enjoy her visits. He loved to listen to our chat and Beryl would always include Bill in the conversation, which I know he appreciated. She would also bring his favourite chocks. Beryl also visited when he was at the hospital, she would surprise him, and he loved it. Bill had a soft spot for Beryl.

Don my brother would visit at home. He made Bill laugh so much, and he needed this therapy, as my darling had not lost his wonderful sense of humour. Joan and Reg would pop up from Dorset; unfortunately dear Reg died a couple of years before Bill.

Only weeks before, we had all enjoyed a meal in a restaurant together, a lovely picture was taken of Reg and Bill shaking hands. It was their last time together and it seemed as if they both new. They were such good friends over the years, and good brothers-in-law.

Reg and Bill—Their Last Farewell

A plaque is inserted on Swanage Pier remembering them both two wonderful men. Swanage was the ideal place as this is where Bill, Reg and all of us spent so many happy times there years ago when we lived in Dorset.

When Betty and Don visited, Betty would love to give Bill grapes. She always made sure they were washed before hand. Dear Betty, she was suffering from Alzheimer's disease. Bill never knew. Betty has sadly now left us.

Neighbours would pop in. Dorothy was always there for us both and is still a good friend to me. Bill was always pleased to see her. Jean would pop in and another Bill Smith who lived opposite would be there to see Bill regularly. They were about the same age.

The two Bills built the conservatory together, and were very good friends. George Keefe was another good friend; he helped me a lot with shopping, putting the bins out and so much more. Sadly George is now no longer with us.

Bill's joy was when a young family of girls popped in. They would wave on their way to school. A couple are now out to work, but it continues as I still have the pleasure of a wave as they pass by.

## CHAPTER FIFTEEN

Time went on, and Bill was beginning to have added problems with his health. In 1994 Bill had another stroke and was admitted to the Royal South Hants Hospital. It was Lesley's 40th birthday so we will never forget this day.

Ryan and Elliott had spent time late in the evening nailing posters with enlarged pictures of Lesley through the ages onto the trees surrounding the close. They were coming into the house as she left to go to the hospital with her dad, and in the flurry she did not notice.

It was sad, as she could not enjoy the day that had been planned for her, but the neighbours enjoyed some laughs at Lesley's pictures as a little girl. Bill stayed in hospital for a couple of weeks and little things along the way began to deteriorate. It was a very gradual process.

My darling also suffered from an enlarged prostate but unfortunately could not have an operation. He really needed it but with the stroke it would have been fatal. A choice was offered, treatment in tablet form with padding—which would only help in a small way—or to be catheterised. The specialist could not help in any other way.

Bill decided after we returned home to talk it over and he opted for the catheter. It made life a lot easier for him not constantly having to go to the toilet it, and enabled him to rest more at night. So for a while life became a little more tolerable for him and also I did not have to empty his bottle several times a night—but I must emphasise I did not mind this at all.

Whatever was good for Bill was all that mattered. The catheter eventually did not agree with Bill, it was constantly being blocked and doctors often had to be called out in the middle of the night to change it. Bill would be in a lot of pain and would be given antibiotics. This unfortunately, continued for the rest of his life.

In between these bouts he was fine, and would get over it and give me a smile, what a fighter! Gradually what with taking so many antibiotics, his immunity came to a stop and the drugs did not do anything for the infection he had. There was nothing we could do except watch and feel sad. After the pains subsided and he felt a little better my dear Bill would stick up his thumb to say that all was well. What a wonderful courageous man, not thinking of himself but to make sure I felt better about it. I tried desperately to mask my anguish, but my darling knew I was suffering mentally with him.

The Twilight nurses and Carers were wonderful. In the early years, carers would come in the morning and shower Bill while he sat on the bath seat. I would help him out of bed but gradually the duties increased and he needed more help.

I was able to walk Bill out into the garden where he would sit and enjoy the sunshine. On one birthday when he was 82 years old, Mac, a friend of ours, built a beautiful waterfall. Bill so enjoyed the rippling of the water and the birds perching on the fall to have a bath. When he was too unwell to go into the garden, we would make it possible for him to look out of the window. The best vantage point for him was the bedroom, and so this became a nightly ritual.

After his evening meal I would help him to wash and get into his pyjamas, we would then sit together until the twilight nurse arrived this would be about 9pm. There was always laughter zooming down from the bedroom. Bill had a wonderful sense of humour and it was wonderful to hear.

This was obviously whilst Bill was fairly well. He really loved the nurses and appreciated all that they did for him. His thanks would show in his eyes and the grip of his hand.

Going back over the years before Bill had so many added problems, Doctor Nightingale advised us both that we should have respite to enable me to have a break and recharge my batteries. This would also be good for Bill. I hated the thought and would only consent to one week every two months.

Lesley and I were invited to look over the Western Hospital. It was a new hospital and we liked what we saw. Bill would have his own room and bathroom and I could be with him whenever I liked. The big problem was telling Bill, we knew he did not want to go.

Eventually a male and female nurse visited him at home to encourage him and give him confidence. They offered to take him to go and see it. I would not have cared if he didn't go, I was quite happy for him to stay at home, but my doctor then put it to me that if I did not get a break I probably wouldn't be fit to look after Bill.

The day came for Bill to go. We went with him in the ambulance and settled him in. A male nurse attended him that day and he was brilliant with us all, not only was Bill insecure I was as well.

After leaving lots of information about Bill's likes and dislikes which was dully pinned on his notice board, we finally had to go. I could not settle at all and would ring in the middle of the night to see if all was well with him. What a pain I must have been, the nurses were very good though, and understood.

It was so hard to let go. I knew how stressed Bill would get if he slipped down in the bed. He had to be propped up at all times. Many times panic attacks would happen at home followed by an asthma attack. Bill had a buzzer to press, but although it was so simple, his brain did not seem to react to it. It took several respite admissions before I settled myself. He was well looked after and was in a happy environment. Every day he would have a visit from Nickie, his carer, to see if there was anything he needed and to bring his washing home as well as take him some goodies.

I visited, but not daily in the beginning. I was told to keep away and have a rest. It was hard but I became more relaxed knowing someone was going in each day. After a few years the respite needed extending as Bill had had the occasional small stroke and was getting frailer. As a result it was updated to a two-week period for every six weeks and this proved to be an asset, as I would be well rested for Bills return.

He so disliked leaving home and we would have a bad day before he went but he was happy while he was there. The nurses were very friendly and they had got to know him very well over the years. He was able use his electric wheel chair, which enabled him to be independent. He could buzz around the grounds and corridors and it made him very happy.

Respite care became invaluable. I was able to have much needed operations over the years on the bladder and bowel and also had my gallbladder removed. I would recoup at the Fenwick in Lyndhurst. Lesley would often have 'Carers Leave' to look after her dad and was able to bring Bill to the along to see me getting better.

Another time I had to an operation on my knee. It was many years ago when I had the kneecap removed. This time I needed keyhole surgery to help the joint as it was deteriorating badly. When I returned home Lesley was there for both of us. A sitting service was eventually set up. Nickie and Celia would sit with him a couple of hours a week and I could then continue to go shopping with Lesley.

**The Millennium.**

The year 2000 was upon us and gradually the world was bursting with spectacular events. On television, the B.B.C reached its pinnacles with wonderful coverage from Tonga that was first to bring in the New Year with singing and dancing. They were followed by Australia with a fantastic fireworks display—it seemed to go on forever and ever.

Gradually we were unconsciously celebrating as we surveyed the world whilst patiently waiting for England's Big Ben Clock to strike on the hour.

Sydney Harbour Bridge and The Opera House portrayed a giant show with massive firework displays.

Palestine released 2000 doves.

The B.B.C had a 27 hour-long extravaganza.

At last it was here, the beginning of a new century. The 1st of January 2000 and we are embarking into the next millennium.

New beginnings, and looking back on past memories and achievements—one of which was the purpose built, 160 foot tall Millennium Dome situated in Greenwich, London. Situated on the south of the river Thames, it would be the setting of a breath-taking extravaganza to herald in the dawn of the new century. It all came together and was finished just days before the big event began.

The Queen and Prince Phillip, along with many celebrities were there for the opening and ended up singing the traditional 'Auld Lang Syne.

10,000 special guest greeted the Millennium with 20,000 thousand bottles of champagne, and 100 gallons of artificial snow fell on the audience creating a life-like blizzard.

The Queen officially declared the £758million centrepiece of Britain open in a live ceremony beamed by satellite to a hundred countries, and 39 tons of fireworks exploded over the London sky. It will be the venue of events and shows for the world to see.

Southampton General Hospital was highlighted showing the Casualty Dept with the staff who worked hard all through the night, and one of them was Lesley my daughter who was a receptionist in the department. A twin was born at 1am, it was magic.

The next day was relatively quiet, as people were probably sleeping late. I did hear a bird or two singing—maybe they were celebrating. Two little snowdrops in my garden poked their heads through welcoming the new century.

The telephones were constantly ringing with New Year greetings. The daily papers arrived with special greetings too, and I managed to get a message inserted for my family, our first wishes for them in the New Century.

The new century unfortunately did not bring joy to Bill, as his health began to deteriorate.

More care was needed, and carers came at teatime. Bill was then helped to wash and dress for bed, ready for the twilight nurses in the evening. A hoist was installed to transfer him into his bed. .

It was so sad that in the last two years of his life he became so poorly. So much care was needed and his dignity was stripped. He suffered so much pain. Fortunately he would sleep a lot as he was so worn out.

A new team of carers were formed as at this time Nickie had moved on to a higher position. They were Julie, Vicky, Patsy, Helen, Donna, Marcia, Jenny, Lyn, and Kelly and Bill loved them. They looked after him so well and took away any embarrassment he felt. It entailed a lot of hard work and I appreciated it so much as it enabled me to keep my Bill with me.

The dreaded day came when he lost the power of his right leg so could not help with the transfers from chair to wheelchair to stair lift. Bill was to be admitted straight away and I pleaded with my G.P for him to be admitted to the Western Hospital. This was not the usual procedure but Doctor Nightingale sorted it for us and we were able to get a bed. It was helpful that Bill had previously received care from the hospital over the years, and now at least he would be with people who knew him.

Bill was very poorly for the next six weeks and I spent as much time with him as I possibly could. The family would pop in and out too. Julie, his carer, was also able to visit daily and see to his needs. Bill always had us around. Julie was great with Bill and also gave support to the family.

As time went on my poor darling was unable to swallow properly and was on soft and liquid foods. I would try to be there for most meals so that I could feed him. Lesley would take and collect me when she was not at work, and so she too was able to see her dad and have some quiet moments with him. Graham, Elliott and Ryan also helped when they were able to.

I managed to write about Bills life, printed it out with pictures and collated it. Visitors and staff would glance through and were able to converse with Bill about his life which was good for encouraging him to communicate. He would join in with smiles, laughs and facial expressions and it certainly was invaluable when he was in hospital.

Most days he would be sleeping quite a lot and then at times he would be bright. We would sit together and I would read the paper to him or softly smooth his head and quietly sing. He liked that.

He loved the picture of Graham, Ryan, and Elliott that was stuck on his cupboard door and would point for visitors to look and smile.

I recall a Saturday, one week before he died. It was one of his better days and I asked if he would like me to push him to the dining room for lunch. He agreed and the patients and staff were pleased to see him. It was quiet and we went into the small room with one table for six and one for two. We chose a table for two, as I didn't think it would have been fair for him to share another table. We had come this far and I was so pleased because ever since he had been unwell he was having all of his meals in his room.

While sitting there and making small talk with Bill and some of the patients, a nurse popped over to me and asked if I would like some fish and chips as they had plenty over. I appreciated that she had asked me and said I would love some. Bill was also pleased. He so loved to know that I was being looked after—always the thoughtful lovely man, even when feeling so poorly.

In came his mushy food and I gave him help to eat it, and then my meal arrived. Bill loved fish and chips and he looked longingly at my plate. I explained why he could not have it and he understood. I wanted the nurse to take it away, but Bill was insistent that I should eat it.

Anyhow while I was talking to the nurse, his hand shot out and he took the biggest chip he could find. He dangled it in front of me—he so wanted it. Of course I said I wish I could give him the lot but he would choke if that chip went into his mouth, then I softened and explained that if he was very careful and just sucked on it maybe it would soften and he could get it down.

He was a very sensible man and I knew he would not do anything foolhardy. We took it in stages, and yes—my darling had his chip. I watched him like a hawk. It took him a long time to devour, but he had savoured every moment and was content enough to not want anymore. And then we both giggled and giggled. It was our secret. I am so glad we had that moment, so glad I had those fish and chips, as he wasn't with me for long after that.

Bill steadily got worse, sleeping most of the time. I did not realise how ill he was as he had gone along this road so many times and bounced back. Elliott visited one day when Bill was very unwell; I wished he hadn't seen him like that as the next day he was so much better.

An appointment was made as the Consultant wanted to see Lesley and me. I was not prepared for what he was about to say, he wanted Bill to move on to a nursing home to be cared for. I was horrified—in no way could I let this happen. He suggested that we should look around. This was the last thing that I wanted to happen. I understood that he could not stay at the Western Hospital indefinitely, but I wanted him to come home for me to nurse him.

The consultant said that this could not happen, as I would not be able to cope. I argued and said that I could as I had been doing it for eleven years, and was still able. I was very adamant. He explained that Bill had lost the use of both legs and he could no longer bear weight. It would need two carers night and day to see to all his needs and this was not available for us. His body was gradually breaking down and in the end I would not be able to cope. It would also not be fair to Bill, as I would be depriving him of all the extra special care he would need. I was truly devastated what was the answer for me? It was definitely not what I had just heard. What was I to do?

## CHAPTER SIXTEEN

Lesley and I duly visited the nursing homes, but none of them met the standard that we wanted for Bill. We reported back to the Consultant and he said, "Keep trying". Oh dear, we were so upset. What was our next step? We were advised by someone in the medical world to prolong it as long as possible, so we had to play the game. We continued our search and actually found one that would maybe suit our requirements. Would this be the way forward?

I would be able to be with Bill all day, but the nighttime was our worry. The door of his room would have to be closed at night under the fire regulations. I was horrified—no way could this dear man be shut in. If he slid down in the bed, he would go into a panic and could not communicate with anyone to let him or her know. As I said before, he could not take onboard how to press a button for the nurse. So this had to be abandoned.

Whatever was our next step? It was decided not do anything, plus our time was needed with Bill—this was more important.

I had made up my mind that at our next appointment with the consultant I would plead with him to let Bill stay. I had done this once before and I was sure I could do it again. The nursing staff agreed with us too, they were all very fond of Bill but they were also aware of the system—they could do nothing to help.

I had many sleepless nights trying to sort out a solution and I decided that if I could not have him at home, I would fight to keep him there. They could not forcibly discharge him, so I would play along as long as I could and keep quiet. If I could maybe do this last thing for my darling, to enable him to stay where his needs were understood in a place that was the next best thing to home, I would be happy. The time when we were seeing the consultant again was near, it was arranged for Wed 3rd Oct. I was ready to see him and plead.

I would face each day as it came along, I never knew what I was going to see or hear when I went into Bill in the mornings, sometimes he would be very poorly. After a bad night he would be sleeping in bed and when awake was not interested in anything around television etc. Another day he would be in his wheelchair as bright as could be, and a big smile would break out when he saw me.

The good days became less and less, he suffered so much with the wretched catheter and so many infections would attack him. The pain would come spasmodic and his facial expressions would say it all. It was horrible to watch knowing there was nothing I could do. Thank goodness whilst in hospital the doctor could give him a jab, put him to sleep and out of pain.

Barbara and Dereck visited at this stage, he smiled, as he knew recognised them and beckoned for Dereck to get a chair for Barbara even though he was so very ill. They were about to visit America for a few weeks but this was the last time they would see their uncle.

One particular day, when I arrived I found his bed empty and he was not around in his usual spots. I quietly panicked. Eventually I saw a nurse and asked if Bill was about. I did not expect her reply. "Oh yes," she said, "he has been wheeled down to the day room". Apparently, when asked, he indicated that he would like to go.

I was amazed, Bill liked to stay in his room or go anywhere but the day room. It was a lovely bright and homely room with plenty of space. Unfortunately he didn't like sitting amongst the other patients, because he would not be able to communicate with them.

I will never know why he agreed to go on this particular day, but better things were to come, as when I arrived at the day-room, who should be sitting in his wheelchair at the top of the room, but my Bill—facing all the other patients on each side.

Pam, the nurse, was giving them some quality time and they were actually playing a game of skittles. She had put the skittles up in the middle of the room and one by one she would hand a plastic ball to the elderly man or lady who would throw it to see how many they could knock down. She had a blackboard at the other end of the room to where Bill was sitting, and chalked up their names to record their scores.

I crept up behind Bill and stroked his head. I was so elated at what I saw—he had bounced back yet once again. A big grin spread across his face, he was so pleased to see me. We held hands and he tightly squeezed mine until it hurt but I would not let go. I was so elated at what I saw. I was so happy.

His turn came to throw the ball. He was a bit reluctant, so I gently encouraged him. It was sad, he had no energy whatsoever and just managed to let it go, but we laughed it off and the game continued. I was so happy, Bill was so bright—was he on the mend once again? Was he again fooling us like he had done on previous setbacks? Would he get well enough to come back home?

My hopes were already rising I would soon be planning his homecoming. The nurse said that he had not been drinking, and I was asked to encourage him. I did manage to get a little into him so we were pleased. He kept looking at me, squeezing my hand and smiling. These were wonderful moments and I treasure them.

It wasn't for long, as those terrible spasms came and he was in so much pain. I asked the nurse if he could go back to his room. I knew he would want to be out of the way without the other patients seeing him in such trouble and hopefully he would feel better in a few minutes.

Unfortunately this time he didn't. His catheter had blocked as it had done so many times and the nurses had to remove it. He was screaming—this was so unusual.

They rushed out of his room for the doctor and I quickly popped in to comfort him. He looked so distressed, I witnessed lots of blood, and before I could cuddle Bill the doctor was there and I was ushered out. He was given morphine, and after a while the doctor came to me and said it would be better if I went home, as Bill would be sleeping a long time. I popped in to see him and he was in a contented sleep, so I left upset and dejected, but pleased that he was out of pain.

Lesley and Ryan were coming to visit with Ringo the dog. Bill and the patients loved to see Ringo and he loved Bill. I met them outside and advised them not to pop in as he had had a bad experience and was sleeping. They took me food shopping but I was upset at what had happened and I wanted to get home. When I eventually returned home a call was on my answer phone to ring the ward, which I did. All was O.K.

Bill had had another little hiccup after I left, but all was well. I wanted to go and see him but they said he was heavily sedated and needed the rest. I rang again later and got the same reply. Thank goodness the doctors were able to help in this way that I was unable to do at home.

Eventually I went to bed and rang them again with the promise that if he was in any distress, I could go straight to him. They agreed and said that the doctor had been round and all was well. He was sleeping peacefully, so I was content knowing how my Bill always bounced back. I went to bed to have a good night's sleep and be up early to visit for hopefully another quality day with my Bill.

It wasn't to be.

At midnight the telephone rang and I had a message from the hospital to say that Bill had died.

It could not be. I had an appointment that very afternoon to see the consultant about Bill staying and to ask more questions. I was devastated and terribly upset and numb, it could not be true, was I dreaming? Lesley and Graham were quickly by my side.

We all tried to comfort one another, it was the most terrible time of my life, I had to compose myself and we had to get to the hospital to be with Bill. This was so important.

It was very quiet as we silently arrived at his room, there was my darling lying in his bed asleep, not as I always saw him, and he was laying down this time, not propped up. At last he was at peace, the tiredness gone from his lovely face, he looked so serene.

His battle was over.

In my grief I was so pleased for him but so terribly sad at my great loss. We stayed with Bill all night they were precious moments. Ryan joined us, we chatted laughed and cried and cuddled Bill all through the night with our memories, those hours went by so quickly.

Graham went to fetch Elliott, but unfortunately he could not face it, such a pity as he would have had so much comfort with his Grandpa, but we understood his grief. The nursing staff continuously brought us tea and we were privileged to stay so many hours with our precious possession. When the day staff came on duty they were so shocked to learn that Bill had died and many of the nurses showed their emotions, it was not expected.

At 9am it was time for Bill to leave, we had our last kiss and cuddle. I was ushered into the sister's office.

As Bill was taken away, Lesley kissed her dad goodbye for the last time—his face was warm and wet with our tears and cuddles. She took the sad journey of seeing him out of the hospital without us.

I was born to love him forever. It has left me with a great void and I cannot remember much about the days that followed. We arranged a lovely funeral for Bill and all who new him were invited to say their farewells.

As a family we held our heads high and proudly walked behind his coffin our hearts tearing to pieces. The Crematorium was packed with people: friends, relatives old work colleagues, nurses and carers. Jackie McAuliffe played three melodious tunes on the piano.

As we sadly walked into the chapel, "The wind beneath my Wings" played quietly on the piano keys in the background.

Our favourite tune from when we first met: "Forgotten Dreams", was softly played throughout the committal.

"No Regrets" was played as the congregation left.

A reception was held at Lesley and Graham's house and about sixty and more people attended. Teresa and Trevor organised an excellent buffet. Gold Balloons were released in the sky, and we waved our farewells as we celebrated the life of a wonderful and courageous man.

## CHAPTER SEVENTEEN

Bill is laid to rest in the lovely woods of the Southampton Crematorium, alongside Mum and pop, and Peter and Marion. It is a beautiful sight in the autumn, and surrounded by crocus and daffodils in the spring.

My lovely husband of fifty-five years -
God Bless Him he will never be forgotten.

I am eternally grateful for the love he gave me, and our family and will be for the rest of my life. It enables me to carry on with my memories that will never be dispelled by time. I know that irrevocably a mist may conceal them from me, but our spirits will be together when that time arrives.

Life will still go on but it will never be the same.
My darling has left a big void in my heart.

He was just 'My Bill'

So Now You Know

The Present—Graham—Elliott—Lesley—Ryan—Me

1789692

Made in the USA